Reading for the Write Reasons

English Reading and Writing for Advanced ESL Students

Donna Aziz-Canuel
Collège Lionel Groulx

Lynne Gaetz
Collège Lionel Groulx

Richard Pawsey
Collège Lionel Groulx

Prentice Hall Regents Canada, Scarborough, Ontario

This book is dedicated to our students, families and friends, for their continued inspiration and support.

Donna Aziz-Canuel

Lynne Gaetz

Richard Pawsey

Canadian Cataloguing in Publication Data

Canuel, Donna Aziz,
Reading for the write reasons

ISBN 0-13-651282-8

1. English language – Textbooks for second language learners.*
I. Gaetz, Lynne, date. II. Pawsey, Richard, date. III. Title.

PE1128 . C35 1996 428 . 2'4 C96-931394-2

Prentice-Hall, Inc., Englewood Cliffs, New Jersey
Prentice-Hall International (UK) Limited, London
Prentice-Hall of Australia, Pty. Limited, Sydney
Prentice-Hall Hispanoamericana, S.A., Mexico City
Prentice-Hall of India Private Limited, New Delhi
Prentice-Hall of Japan, Inc., Tokyo
Simon & Schuster Asia Private Limited, Singapore
Editora Prentice-Hall do Brasil, Ltda., Rio de Janeiro

ISBN 0-13-651282-8

Acquisitions Editor: Dominique Roberge
Managing Editor: Marta Tomins
Senior Editor: Imogen Brian
Copy Editor: Vivien Young
Production Coordinator: Sharon Houston
Permissions Research: Marijke Leupen
Cover and Interior Design: Gail Ferreira Ng-A-Kien
Cover Image: Marc Mongeau

1 2 3 4 5 HP 01 00 99 98 97

Printed and bound in the United States

Contents

	Preface	*vii*
	Writer's Tool Box	*ix*
	Technical Checklist	*x*
Chapter 1	**Life and Literature**	**1**
	Pre-Reading	1
	Essay — "The Best Training for Real Life — Fiction" by Michael Korda	2
	Vocabulary and Comprehension	3
	Oral Discussion	4
	Writing Challenge	5
Chapter 2	**The Essay Genre**	**7**
	Pre-Reading	8
	Essay — "Finishing School" by Maya Angelou	8
	Vocabulary and Comprehension	12
	Oral Discussion	12
	Tools of the Trade — Focus on the Topic Sentence	12
	Writing Challenge	16
Chapter 3	**Descriptive Writing**	**17**
	Pre-Reading	17
	Essay — "The Discus Thrower" by Richard Selzer	18
	Vocabulary and Comprehension	21
	Oral Discussion	21
	Poem — "Do Not Go Gentle Into That Good Night" by Dylan Thomas	22
	Oral Discussion	22
	Tools of the Trade — A Strong Introduction	23
	Writing Challenge	25
Chapter 4	**Getting Your Message Across**	**27**
	Pre-Reading	27
	Essay — "Hisstory" by Rene Taylor (Ontario)	28
	Vocabulary and Comprehension	30

	Oral Discussion	31
	Tools of the Trade — An Effective Conclusion	31
	Writing Challenge	34
Chapter 5	The Short Story	35
	Pre-Reading	37
	Short Story — "Lamb to the Slaughter" by Roald Dahl	37
	Vocabulary and Comprehension	43
	Oral Activities	45
	Tools of the Trade — Planning an Essay	46
	Writing Challenge	47
Chapter 6	Character Development	49
	Pre-Reading	50
	Short Story — "Monkey On My Back" by Paul L. Vasey (Ontario)	50
	Vocabulary and Comprehension	57
	Oral Discussion	59
	Tools of the Trade — Defining Character	59
	Tools of the Trade — Analyzing Character	61
	Writing Challenge	62
Chapter 7	Setting	63
	Pre-Reading	63
	Short Story — "Gold Wings" by Leo McKay Jr. (Nova Scotia)	64
	Vocabulary and Comprehension	69
	Oral Discussion	71
	Oral Activity	71
	Tools of the Trade — Analyzing Setting	71
	Poem — "On Saint-Urbain Street" by Milton Acorn (Quebec)	72
	Vocabulary and Comprehension	73
	Oral Discussion	73
	Writing Challenge	74
Chapter 8	Theme	75
	Pre-Reading	76
	Short Story — "Bugs" by Nancy Holmes (Alberta)	76
	Vocabulary and Comprehension	80
	Oral Discussion	81
	Tools of the Trade — Analyzing Theme	82
	Writing Challenge	83

Chapter 9 Comparison and Contrast 85

Tools of the Trade — The Thesis Statement and Comparison and Contrast 85
Fairy Tale — "Rapunzel" 88
Short Story — "Bad Girl" by David Arnason (Manitoba) 91
Oral Discussion 95
Writing Challenge 95
Essay — "The Birth of Max Mueller — September 26, 1971" by Cookie Mueller 95
Poem — "Stainless Steel Reflections" by M. J. Canuel (Quebec) 99
Oral Discussion 99
Writing Challenge 99

The Oral Presentation 101

Organizing 101
Preparing 102
Presenting 103

Grammar Appendix

Section 1 Subject–Verb Agreement 105
Section 2 The Present Perfect Versus The Simple Past 109
Section 3 The Past Perfect Versus The Simple Past 115
Section 4 Pronoun Pitfalls 119
Section 5 Punctuating to Avoid Fragments and Run Ons 125
Section 6 Using Quotation Marks and Citing References 131
Section 7 Sentence Problems 137
Section 8 Spelling Pitfalls 143
Section 9 Gallicisms 151

Acknowledgments

We would like to thank the following people for their continued help and support in allowing us to grow with this book: the English Department at Collège Lionel-Groulx; especially Elizabeth Schinkel for her keen eye and good-natured comments, Robert Von Kropp, Heather Yorston, and Sonia Margossian. We are also indebted to Yolanda de Rooy, Cliff Newman, Marta Tomins, Imogen Brian, Dominique Roberge, and Bobbie Smith from Prentice-Hall Canada. We appreciate the useful comments from reviewers Claudia Rock, Collège de Saint Jérôme, and Diane Boisvert and David Oranson, Cégep de Saint-Laurent. We would like to extend special thanks to Paul Fournier for his continued encouragement and sense of humour. Finally, we thank our families and students who helped to keep us sane and focused after we realised what we had gotten ourselves into.

Preface

The title *Reading for the Write Reasons* is a deliberate play on words. As an advanced ESL student, you have already acquired a certain ease in communicating in English, but you have also learned that acquiring a language is an on-going process and that this process is enhanced by exposure to a variety of language situations. This book is aimed at providing you with exposure to one particular language situation: reading. You will read, discuss and write about literature.

What are the ***write*** reasons for reading? How will reading help you to become a more effective writer?

Through reading a selection of essays, short stories, and poems, you will be exposed to:

* challenging vocabulary and its effective use in writing
* elements of literary structure and style, and their impact on writing
* the transformation of ideas into literary form

You will also be asked to discuss and write about these readings. The **Writer's Tool Box** will give you effective writing strategies and organizational skills. In each chapter except the first one, you will be exposed to a specific strategy for effective writing. As the book progresses, collect these tools in the Writer's Tool Box which follows the Preface. It will help you prepare and organize your own future writing.

An indispensable part of writing is editing. The points covered in the **Grammar Appendix** are based on the needs of most advanced ESL learners. After a brief explanation of the grammar point in question, there are exercises designed to identify and edit incorrect usage. Use the grammar points covered in the Appendix to construct a **Technical Checklist** which will help you with proofreading your own writing. The Technical Checklist also follows the Preface.

What are the ***right*** reasons for reading? Why is it important to read?

Reading for the Write Reasons is more than just the title of this book, it is the philosophy on which it is based. The book starts with a reading that begs the question *what is literature and what role does it play in my life?* All the readings that follow have been selected in the spirit of this question. They represent a wide variety of writing styles and periods (from traditional favorites to *avant garde,* little-known writers), themes (from birth to death, and everything else in between), perspectives (from that of a recent immigrant to that of a gay teacher). While it is impossible that all the readings will touch you in the same way, every student using this book will be able to see a bit of themselves in the experiences of at least some of the writers.

All the material in this book has been class tested to the enjoyment of students in a Quebec College. It is our hope that you will enjoy it as much as we have.

WRITER'S TOOL BOX

List below all the self-help questions designed to improve the stylistic aspects of your writing.

	YES	NO
1. ____________	____	____
2. ____________	____	____
3. ____________	____	____
4. ____________	____	____
5. ____________	____	____
6. ____________	____	____
7. ____________	____	____
8. ____________	____	____
9. ____________	____	____
10. ____________	____	____

TECHNICAL CHECKLIST

List below all the self-help questions designed to improve the technical aspects of your writing.

		YES	NO
1.	________	____	____
2.	________	____	____
3.	________	____	____
4.	________	____	____
5.	________	____	____
6.	________	____	____
7.	________	____	____
8.	________	____	____
9.	________	____	____
10.	________	____	____

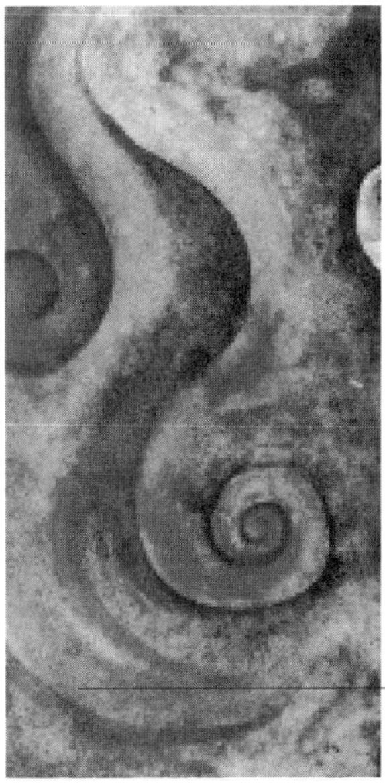

CHAPTER 1

Life and Literature

Literature plays a role in life, and life plays a role in literature. In everyday life, you express your thoughts about events that have moved you, irritated you, humored you, or even humiliated you. Art is created by our interpretation of these events. As a writer you use words the same way other artists use their tools. Sculptors have knives and clay; painters have brushes and paint; musicians have notes and instruments. The writer has words. The next few chapters will concentrate on giving you strategies to use your primary tool — words.

PRE-READING

Before you read the text below, consider the following:

1. Think of a book, a movie or a song that has left a strong and lasting impression on you. Why was the effect so powerful?
2. Why is it relevant to read literature?
3. Why should all students be exposed to literature?

THE BEST TRAINING FOR REAL LIFE – FICTION

by Michael Korda

1 Literature — good, bad and indifferent — shapes our lives. When we are young, it is the stuff of our dreams, fantasies and ambitions, not only an escape from the far less interesting real world around us, but also a way of learning about things that all too often can't be learned at home. A child of divorced parents and far-flung relatives, I made a family of the Rostovs, in *War and Peace*, because they were everything my own family was not — close-knit, emotional, living for each other.

2 Psychologists suppose that *life* teaches us what we know, for better or worse, but it's most often from fiction that we form our attitudes about life. If we waited for life to teach us about romantic love, for example, we might never learn anything about it at all — we pick that up, early on, from romantic novels, whether they're by Emily Brontë, Jane Austen or Danielle Steel. It's to books, movies and TV that we turn, in childhood and adolescence, for information about love, feelings, relationships in the adult world, and when we ourselves inevitably *become* adults, what we have learned from those sources becomes part of us, part of the way we see life — more important, part of the way we see *ourselves*.

3 A generation of young Americans modeled themselves after — or at least saw themselves reflected in — Holden Caulfield, or Franny and Zooey, in much the same way that ten years later the attitude of young Americans toward war was radically altered by reading *Catch-22*, or toward drugs was changed by reading *On the Road.* Books provide not only role models, they also teach us lessons we never forget about courage, sacrifice, ambition and desire, right and wrong, love and hate, war and peace.

4 All the lessons of life are there, buried in great books and great drama, and the interesting thing is that we absorb them without a sense of being *taught*, without effort, for at the same time we are being entertained. Time spent reading is therefore never, under any circumstances, time wasted, provided that what we're reading is worthwhile.

5 I'm sometimes astonished to realize how much of my own perceptions of life are filtered through literature. If I hadn't been exposed to Hemingway, T.E. Lawrence and Orwell at an early age, I wouldn't have left college in 1956 to go fight in the Hungarian Revolution, and if I hadn't been sustained there by the notion that what I was doing was essentially a romantic, literary act, I don't think I would have survived. If I hadn't read about the grandeurs of the military life, I would certainly not have joined the British armed forces when I was 17, nor been able to look upon that experience as interesting and significant, rather than a painful and time-wasting episode of three years duration, as my family viewed it.

6 When you come right down to bedrock, Shakespeare tells us more about jealousy in *Othello* than we are ever likely to find out by reading a modern nonfiction bestseller on the subject, and Dickens tells us more about families than we are ever going to learn from the works of modern family counselors. Literature is not an *escape* from life, it is a way of *experiencing* life, on a larger scale — a way of understanding that what we feel and experience has been felt and experienced before, that our problems are not unique but have been faced by other people, and overcome.

7 That, in the end, is the most important lesson of literature: that we are *not alone* in suffering the problems of childhood, or adolescence, or love, or marriage, or pain, or even

death; that others over the centuries have gone through the same things and survived. In real life, it is hard to find people who can talk to us about such things — or at any rate who can talk to us sensibly, frankly and openly, beyond the usual clichés — but literature is full of just such experiences, from which anybody who can read, can *learn*.

8 In the end, great literature teaches us about *ourselves*. It does *not* offer us pat, ready-made solutions, like self-help books; it offers examples and life experiences that help us, in good times or bad, to face our own problems.

9 It is one of the ironies of our present age that increasingly we trust only what is new, based on "research," whereas the real truths almost always lie elsewhere. The works of self-help gurus, in the end, are thin fodder compared to Tolstoy, Dickens and Balzac, or their more modern equivalents, to the extent there are any. How many people do we know in this new age of materialism (which in so many ways resembles the Twenties) who remind us of Gatsby, desperately trying to compensate for his inner emptiness with glitzy material success? I can never reread *Gatsby* without thinking of the number of people I know who are having a lousy time in the middle of their own prosperity and success today, and who don't know *why*, despite the fact that F. Scott Fitzgerald understood it perfectly, and wrote about it better than anyone else.

10 Circumstances change, customs and habits die out and are replaced by others, but human nature doesn't change, and hence literature is never out of date. That is why *King Lear* still tells us all we need to know about the perils of old age and pride, and why *Oedipus* still reads as if it had been written yesterday.

11 When I was a child, I was often told not to spend so much time sitting by myself with a book. How would I learn anything about life, I was warned, if I spent it reading? As a child, I took these warnings seriously, though I managed to keep on doing just what I wanted to do much of the time. But now, decades later, I can see that the advice was wrong. I learned far more about life from reading books than I would have from playing in the park or tossing a ball around with other children.

12 What lessons I did learn in the park and on the playing fields I have long since forgotten, or have been disproved by experience. The lessons I learned from books have stayed with me — and have invariably proved to be true.

VOCABULARY AND COMPREHENSION

1. Define the following words or expressions in the context in which they are used from the essay "The Best Training for Life—Fiction" by Michael Korda.

   a. *far-flung relatives* (par. 1) ______________________________

   b. *When you come right down to bedrock* (par.6) ______________________________

   c. *pat* (par. 8) ______________________________

   d. *thin fodder* (par. 9) ______________________________

2. A **synonym** is a word that is similar in meaning to another word. Find three synonyms for the word *hence.*

   a. ______________________________

   b. ______________________________

   c. ______________________________

3. In paragraph 9 of his essay, Michael Korda says:

   "It is one of the *ironies* of our present age that increasingly we trust only what is new, based on 're-search,' whereas the real truths almost always lie elsewhere."

   a. Define irony ____

   b. Why does he see this as being ironic?

   ____

   ____

ORAL DISCUSSION

1. In paragraph 4 of his essay, Michael Korda makes the statement:

   "Time spent reading is therefore never, under any circumstances, time wasted, provided that what we're reading is worthwhile."

   Do you agree with this statement? What constitutes *worthwhile reading?*

2. According to the author:

   "Literature is not an *escape* from life, it is a way of *experiencing* life, on a larger scale—a way of understanding that what we feel and experience has been felt and experienced before, that our problems are not unique but have been faced by other people, and overcome." (par. 6)

   Do you agree with this statement? Why or why not?

3. "In the end, great literature teaches us about *ourselves*. It does *not* offer us pat ready made solutions like self-help books; it offers examples and life experiences that help us, in good times or bad, to face our own problems."

   Based on your experience, do you agree with Korda? Explain your answer.

4. One reader of this essay has summarized it this way:

   LIFE ⟶ LITERATURE ⟶ LIFE

   Do you think this summary is appropriate? Why or why not?

WRITING CHALLENGE

1. a. Write your own definition of literature.
   b. Write a defence for your definition. Include an explanation with reasons.
2. Find a quotation about literature from a well-known writer. Write a text in which you compare the author's perspective to that of Michael Korda.

CHAPTER 2

The Essay Genre

When Montaigne, a French philosopher, published his collection of writings called *Essais* in 1580, he had no idea that his adopted form would endure into the twenty-first century. In the beginning, the **essay** was appreciated for its important subject matter, logical organization, serious tone and moral or educational lesson. Throughout the centuries it has evolved to include a form of writing that is more informal in tone and subject matter, but no less carefully organized. It is possible today for any reader to find ample examples of both type of essays. One need only open a daily newspaper, a history or anthropology text, or even *Rolling Stone Magazine* to see the range in style from the very informal to the highly sophisticated and formal.

What differentiates an essay from other short prose, such as short stories, is that an essay is non-fiction. It is a genre of writing through which an author attempts to motivate readers to think about an idea. In the following chapters, you will read and discuss several essays. Some are informal while others are formal, but you will notice how all the authors rely on a combination of descriptive, narrative (story telling) and expository (opinion) writing skills to illustrate their ideas. Reading and discussing these essays will help to make you a better critical reader and ultimately a better writer.

PRE-READING

In this chapter you will read a complete narrative essay. Before doing so, read the narrative paragraph below, and discuss the questions that follow.

CLEAVAGE

I was ten and I really had no interest in being one of six junior bridesmaids at cousin Connie's wedding. Little did I know that my mother sealed my fate when she accepted on my behalf. The dress affair was a total disaster. The dressmaker decided that my undeveloped ten year old body needed help. "What God has forgotten we'll stuff with cotton," she announced before the entire female half of the wedding party. To make matters worse Mom decided that I would need my first bra to support the cotton. Our sojourn to the teen department resulted in my mother and a rather impatient salesgirl trying to fit a AAA training bra over the coat I had stubbornly refused to remove. The day of the wedding dawned early, and I was padded, prodded and pinned into the blue satin dress. Alas, as I attempted to gracefully glide up the aisle, I looked down to my non-existent cleavage and to my horror saw the strategically placed wads of Kimberly Clarke wending their way up and over the décolleté neck of the dress.

To this day I wince when I look at the pictures.

ORAL EXERCISE

1. In your own words explain in chronological order what happened.
2. Why do you think this paragraph was written in the first person? Would the writer / reader relationship have been different had this been written in the third person?
3. Although the narrator gives very little explicit information about herself, what can you deduce about her personality. Give evidence from the text to support your opinion.

Keep these questions in mind as you read the following essay.

FINISHING SCHOOL

by Maya Angelou

1 Recently a white woman from Texas, who would quickly describe herself as a liberal, asked me about my hometown. When I told her that in Stamps my grandmother had owned the only Negro general merchandise store since the turn of the century, she exclaimed, "Why, you were a debutante." Ridiculous and even ludicrous. But Negro girls in small Southern towns, whether poverty-stricken or just munching along on a few of life's necessities, were given as

extensive and irrelevant preparations for adulthood as rich white girls shown in magazines. Admittedly the training was not the same. While white girls learned to waltz and sit gracefully with a tea cup balanced on their knees, we were lagging behind, learning the mid-Victorian values with very little money to indulge them. . . .

2 We were required to embroider and I had trunkfuls of colorful dishtowels, pillowcases, runners and handkerchiefs to my credit. I mastered the art of crocheting and tatting, and there was a life-time's supply of dainty doilies that would never be used in sacheted dresser drawers. It went without saying that all girls could iron and wash, but the finer touches around the home, like setting a table with real silver, baking roasts, and cooking vegetables without meat, had to be learned elsewhere. Usually at the source of those habits. During my tenth year, a white woman's kitchen became my finishing school.

3 Mrs. Viola Cullinan was a plump woman who lived in a three-bedroom home somewhere behind the post office. She was singularly unattractive until she smiled, and then the lines around her eyes and mouth which made her look perpetually dirty disappeared, and her face looked like the mask of an impish elf. She usually rested her smile until late afternoon when her women friends dropped in and Miss Glory, the cook, served them cold drinks on the closed-in porch.

4 The exactness of her house was inhuman. This glass went here and only here. That cup had its place and it was an act of impudent rebellion to place it anywhere else. At twelve o'clock the table was set. At 12:15 Mrs. Cullinan sat down to dinner (whether her husband had arrived or not). At 12:16 Miss Glory brought out the food.

5 It took me a week to learn the difference between a salad plate, a bread plate, and a dessert plate.

6 Mrs. Cullinan kept up the tradition of her wealthy parents. She was from Virginia. Miss Glory, who was a descendant of slaves that had worked for the Cullinans, told me her history. She had married beneath her (according to Miss Glory). Her husband's family hadn't had their money very long and what they had "didn't 'mount to much."

7 As ugly as she was, I thought privately, she was lucky to get a husband above or beneath her station. But Miss Glory wouldn't let me say a thing against her mistress. She was very patient with me, however, over the housework. She explained the dishware, silverware, and servants' bells. The large round bowl in which soup was served wasn't a soup bowl, it was a tureen. There were goblets, sherbet glasses, ice-cream glasses, wine glasses, green glass coffee cups with matching saucers, and water glasses. I had a glass to drink from, and it sat with Miss Glory's on a separate shelf from the others. Soup spoons, gravy boat, butter knives, salad forks, and carving platter were additions to my vocabulary and in fact almost represented a new language. I was fascinated with the novelty, with the fluttering Mrs. Cullinan and her Alice-in-Wonderland house.

8 Her husband remains, in my memory, undefined. I lumped him with all the other white men that I had ever seen and tried not to see.

9 On our way home one evening, Miss Glory told me that Mrs. Cullinan couldn't have children. She said that she was too delicate-boned. It was hard to imagine bones at all under those layers of fat. Miss Glory went on to say that the doctor had taken out all her lady organs. I reasoned that a pig's organs included the lungs, heart and liver, so if Mrs. Cullinan was walking around without those essentials, it explained why she drank alcohol out of unmarked bottles. She was keeping herself embalmed.

10 When I spoke to Bailey about it, he agreed that I was right, but he also informed me that Mr. Cullinan had two daughters by a coloured lady and that I knew them very well. He added that the girls were the spitting image of their father. I was unable to remember what he looked like, although I had just left him a few hours before, but I thought of the Coleman girls. They were very light-skinned and certainly didn't look very much like their mother (no one ever mentioned Mr. Coleman).

11 My pity for Mrs. Cullinan preceded me the next morning like the Cheshire cat's smile. Those girls, who could have been her daughters, were beautiful. They didn't have to straighten their hair. Even when they were caught in the rain, their braids still hung down straight like tamed snakes. Their mouths were pouty little cupid's bows. Mrs. Cullinan didn't know what she missed. Or maybe she did. Poor Mrs. Cullinan.

12 For weeks after, I arrived early, left late and tried very hard to make up for her barrenness. If she had had her own children, she wouldn't have had to ask me to run a thousand errands from her back door to the back door of her friends. Poor old Mrs. Cullinan.

13 Then one evening Miss Glory told me to serve the ladies on the porch. After I set the tray down and turned toward the kitchen, one of the women asked, "What's your name, girl?" It was the speckled-face one. Mrs. Cullinan said, "She doesn't talk much. Her name's Margaret."

14 "Is she dumb?"

15 "No. As I understand it, she can talk when she wants to but she's usually quiet as a little mouse. Aren't you, Margaret?"

16 I smiled at her. Poor thing. No organs and couldn't even pronounce my name correctly.

17 "She's a sweet little thing, though."

18 "Well, that may be, but the name's too long. I'd never bother myself. I'd call her Mary if I was you."

19 I fumed into the kitchen. That horrible woman would never have the chance to call me Mary because if I was starving I'd never work for her...

20 That evening I decided to write a poem on being white, fat, old and without children. It was going to be a tragic ballad. I would have to watch her carefully to capture the essence of her loneliness and pain.

21 The very next day, she called me by the wrong name. Miss Glory and I were washing up the lunch dishes when Mrs. Cullinan came to the doorway. "Mary?"

22 Miss Glory asked, "Who?"

23 Mrs. Cullinan, sagging a little, knew and I knew. "I want Mary to go down to Mrs. Randall's and take her some soup. She's not been feeling well for a few days."

24 Miss Glory's face was a wonder to see. "You mean Margaret, ma'am. Her name's Margaret."

25 "That's too long. She's Mary from now on. Heat that soup from last night and put it in the china tureen and, Mary, I want you to carry it carefully."

26 Every person I knew had a hellish horror of being "called out of his name." It was a dangerous practice to call a Negro anything that could be loosely construed as insulting because of the centuries of their having been called niggers, jigs, dinges, blackbirds, crows, boots and spooks.

27 Miss Glory had a fleeting second of feeling sorry for me. Then as she handed me the

hot tureen she said, "Don't mind, don't pay that no mind. Sticks and stones may break your bones, but words ... You know, I been working for her for twenty years."

28 She held the back door open for me. "Twenty years. I wasn't much older than you. My name used to be Hallelujah. That's what Ma named me, but my mistress give me 'Glory,' and it stuck. I likes it better too."

29 I was in the little path that ran behind the houses when Miss Glory shouted. "It's shorter too."

30 For a few seconds it was a tossup over whether I would laugh (imagine being named Hallelujah) or cry (imagine letting some white woman rename you for her convenience). My anger saved me from either outburst. I had to quit the job, but the problem was going to be how to do it. Momma wouldn't allow me to quit for just any reason.

31 "She's a peach. That woman is a real peach." Mrs. Randall's maid was talking as she took the soup from me, and I wondered what her name used to be and what she answered to now.

32 For a week I looked into Mrs. Cullinan's face as she called me Mary. She ignored my coming late and leaving early. Miss Glory was a little annoyed because I had begun to leave egg yolk on the dishes and wasn't putting much heart in polishing the silver. I hoped that she would complain to our boss, but she didn't.

33 Then Bailey solved my dilemma. He had me describe the contents of the cupboard and the particular plates she liked best. Her favorite piece was a casserole shaped like a fish and the green glass coffee cups. I kept his instructions in mind, so on the next day when Miss Glory was hanging out clothes and I had again been told to serve the old biddies on the porch, I dropped the empty serving tray. When I heard Mrs. Cullinan scream, "Mary!" I picked up the casserole and two of the green glass cups in readiness. As she rounded the kitchen door I let them fall on the tiled floor.

34 I could never absolutely describe to Bailey what happened next, because each time I got to the part where she fell on the floor and screwed up her ugly face to cry, we burst out laughing. She actually wobbled around on the floor and picked up shards of the cups and cried, "Oh, Momma. Oh, dear Gawd. It's Momma's china from Virginia. Oh, Momma, I sorry."

35 Miss Glory came running in from the yard and the women from the porch crowded around. Miss Glory was almost as broken up as her mistress. "You mean to say she broke our Virginia dishes? What we gone do?"

36 Mrs. Cullinan cried louder. "That clumsy nigger. Clumsy little black nigger."

37 Old speckled-face leaned down and asked. "Who did it, Viola? Was it Mary? Who did it?"

38 Everything was happening so fast I can't remember whether her action preceded her words, but I know that Mrs. Cullinan said, "Her name's Margaret, goddamn it, her name's Margaret." And she threw a wedge of the broken plate at me. It could have been the hysteria which put her aim off, but the flying crockery caught Miss Glory right over her ear and she started screaming.

39 I left the front door wide open so all the neighbors could hear.

40 Mrs. Cullinan was right about one thing. My name wasn't Mary.

VOCABULARY AND COMPREHENSION

1. What is the meaning and the significance of the title *Finishing School?*

   ___

   ___

2. Comment on the atmosphere created by the following line: "The exactness of her house was inhuman." (par. 4)

   ___

   ___

3. A **metaphor** is an indirect comparison of two seemingly different ideas to extend meaning beyond the literal. Explain the metaphor: "She was keeping herself embalmed." (par. 9)

   ___

   ___

4. Carefully consider the various words Angelou uses in reference to Margaret: *negro, niggers, jigs, dinges, blackbirds, crows, boots, spooks, Mary*. Of all of these which word is the cruelest for Margaret? Why?

   ___

   ___

   ___

ORAL DISCUSSION

1. What thesis (central idea) is Maya Angelou prompting her readers to think about in "Finishing School" ?
2. Does Angelou ever explicitly state the main thesis of her essay?
3. How does she make her thesis known to the reader?
4. Why would Angelou choose to tell a story to reveal her thesis rather than explicitly stating it?
5. What are the possible drawbacks of choosing to tell a story?
6. How important is Angelou's characterization of Mrs.Cullinan?

TOOLS OF THE TRADE

Focus on the Topic Sentence

A **topic sentence** states the main point of a paragraph. It is usually the first sentence in a paragraph and tells the reader what the paragraph will be about. It establishes *the focus of the paragraph* and is *interesting enough to make the reader want to keep reading.*

PLANNING A TOPIC SENTENCE

Writing a good topic sentence takes a little bit of planning.

The first thing you have to realize about a topic sentence is that it is the most **general statement** you will make in your paragraph. *Everything that comes after it will be a detail* to support that general statement.

What does this mean in practical terms? Examine the words below.

Cars {
- Porsche Carrera
- Cadillac Seville
- Toyota Tercel
- Suzuki Sidekick
- Mercedes 450 SL

The word *cars* tells you what the *general category* is that you want to talk about and the *five models of cars* listed give you the *details* about that general category.

If you want to write a paragraph using the above information, the first step is to come up with an effective topic sentence. When you decide to take a general category, like cars, and turn it into a topic sentence, you have to consider a number of questions?

Look at the examples below.

a. What if you wrote the following topic sentence?

I like all cars.

Are the five models of cars mentioned enough to support this statement? ☐ Yes ☐ No

In fact, if you really wanted to support the statement *I like all cars,* you would need to talk about almost every kind of car imaginable and this could not be done in one paragraph. As a result, your topic sentence would be *too general.*

b. What if you decided to write this topic sentence?

I like cars that have four-wheel drive.

Could all five models of cars be included in your paragraph? ☐ Yes ☐ No

In fact, the only car listed that has four-wheel drive is the *Suzuki Sidekick,* so your topic sentence would not allow you to mention the four other models of cars. Here your topic sentence is *too specific.*

c. What if you wrote the sentence below?

I like many kinds of cars.

Are the five models of cars mentioned enough to support this statement? ☐ Yes ☐ No

Could all five models of cars be included in your paragraph? ☐ Yes ☐ No

Now consider another important question:

Does the sentence *grab your attention* and make you want to keep reading? ☐ Yes ☐ No

This sentence is not very interesting. The topic sentence is not only there to give the paragraph its focus, it must also grab the attention of the reader.

d. What about this sentence?

Choosing the perfect car can be a matter of taste or a question of budget.

Are the five models of cars mentioned enough to support this statement?	☐ Yes	☐ No
Could all five models of cars be included in your paragraph?	☐ Yes	☐ No
Does the sentence grab your attention and make you want to keep reading?	☐ Yes	☐ No

WRITING A GOOD TOPIC SENTENCE

Look at the following details and write the category to which they belong. Then, try to write a good topic sentence for the category.

General Category	***Details***	***topic sentence:*** ____________________
____________________	grunge	______________________________
	heavy metal	______________________________
	disco	______________________________
	rap	______________________________
	classical	______________________________
		______________________________
		______________________________

Now, study your topic sentence and answer the following questions:

Are the five types of music mentioned enough to support this statement?	☐ Yes	☐ No
Could all five types of music be included in your paragraph?	☐ Yes	☐ No
Does the sentence grab your attention and make you want to keep reading?	☐ Yes	☐ No

If the answer to all three questions is *yes*, then you have a good topic sentence.

HELPFUL STRATEGIES

Examine the following paragraph. You will notice that it does not have a topic sentence. List the details that appear in the paragraph and then decide on a good topic sentence.

____

________________________________. They use them to pick up food but also to spray water, carry things and swat insects. The mother elephant even uses her trunk to help in the raising of her calves. She can give her offspring a hug with it when she is feeling affectionate, or she can use it to spank a calf when it is misbehaving. Also, when there is danger, elephants can use their trunks to make a loud warning noise. So, although they may look weird, elephants' trunks are indispensable.

List the details below. The uses for an elephant's trunk include the following:

1. ____

2. ____

3. ____

4. ____

5. ____

Choose the general category for these details.

☐ elephants

☐ elephants' trunks

☐ the usefulness of elephants' trunks

Now, write your topic sentence at the beginning of the paragraph and ask yourself the following questions to see whether your topic sentence is an effective one:

Is my topic sentence too general?	☐ Yes	☐ No
Is my topic sentence too specific?	☐ Yes	☐ No
Is my topic sentence interesting?	☐ Yes	☐ No

EVERY DETAIL COUNTS

Do not forget that your *topic sentence* is the *focus of your paragraph*. As a result, every detail that comes after your topic sentence should relate to that topic sentence!

Read the following sentence and answer the questions that follow:

When I was young, I didn't appreciate the value of money.

Indicate which sentences would go with this topic sentence and which would not.

My father had a well-paying job so my family was very well provided for.	☐ Yes	☐ No
My mother came from a poor family and did not want to deprive her children in any way. As a result, she always bent over backwards to ensure that we had everything.	☐ Yes	☐ No

I think American money is considerably uglier than Canadian money.	☐ Yes	☐ No
I used to expect that my parents would buy me anything I wanted when I wanted it.	☐ Yes	☐ No
It never occurred to me that someone had to work to earn the money to pay for it.	☐ Yes	☐ No
My father insisted that my bed be made daily and that my room be immaculately clean.	☐ Yes	☐ No
Today, I have four credit cards but I don't use them because the interest charges are far too high.	☐ Yes	☐ No
I learned the value of money as soon as I got my first job.	☐ Yes	☐ No

WRITING CHALLENGE

1. Write a narrative essay in which you describe how your name was chosen for you.
2. Look in a name book or dictionary and describe the meaning of your name. Do you believe that the definition of your name reflects your personality?
3. Relate an experience when you either thought about changing or actually changed your name.
4. Narrative essays tell a story and answer the question, "What happened?" Write a narrative about a *significant* event from your past. The reason for the significance should be made clear throughout your narrative.

> The following question now has significance for you.
> Add it to the **Writer's Tool Box** at the beginning of your book.
>
> **HAVE I WRITTEN AN EFFECTIVE TOPIC SENTENCE?**

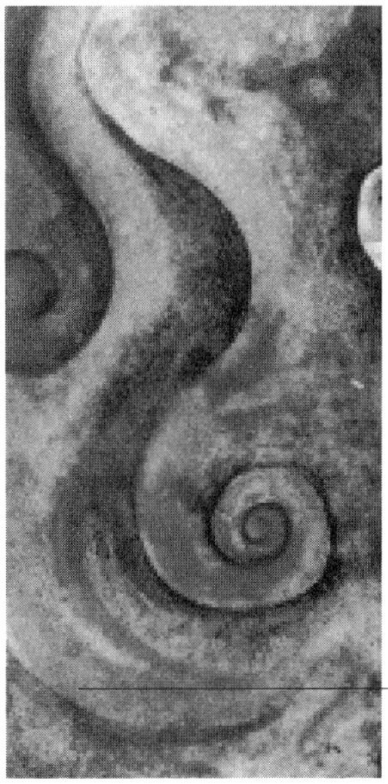

CHAPTER 3

Descriptive Writing

When you experience a moment in life, your impressions are formed by your senses. When you read or write about these experiences, you are creating a virtual reality based on how well you can imagine and use those senses. Your imaginings take shape through the use of words. Because words cannot see, taste, smell, hear or feel on their own, you have to combine words to create these sensations and make the words come alive for the reader.

PRE-READING

In this chapter you will be reading a descriptive essay. Before doing so, read the following descriptive paragraph, and discuss the questions that follow.

SHARING SECRETS

I thought to myself, "Damn that Conrad is a good writer," as I tossed the book onto the floor next to my bed and reached for my nightly glass of grapefruit juice. I clicked onto CNN to check what was happening IRL (that's *In Real Life* for those of you who are uninitiated to the Net) and sipped at the bitter fruit re-constituted drink and settled back for my daily dose of brutal reality. There was droning about budgets and Congress, White House chicanery and similar reports of moo-moo droppings and I was set to drift off into the nether regions of sleep when an item came up on some man who had spent his life virtually alone in a house from which he seldom ventured. He had plastered every square inch of every wall in his house with clippings from newspapers. What made this story even more bizarre was that each room had a particular theme. The kitchen had been reserved for the classifieds, the living room for editorials, and the bathroom obviously had the comic section. The man in question was almost unknown to his neighbors who showed interest more in their moment in the limelight than in the peculiarity of this man's life. I wondered what could have driven a person to do such a thing. To spend so much of his life doing something so utterly senseless, as though he were looking for order in his life, and that from the search and commitment for this order he had found a meaning for his life. And after all who were we to comment on this. I reached down and picked up my discarded book and rushed through some of the pages which could parallel this man's life, and at that moment as I read them I saw how Marlowe and Kurtz and their descent into the heart of darkness was the story of every man. Including yours truly. I turned the pages looking for passages which I thought might relate and as I scanned them I let slip a mild expletive or two. It was as though each line was about that man, and I thought to myself again, damn what a good book this is, and what a genius Conrad had to be. I turned back to page one and started over with enthusiasm, removing layer after layer of gauze from this work, searching for its heart of darkness.

ORAL EXERCISE

Look back at the paragraph you have just read and answer the questions below.

1. Which senses are appealed to? (smell, taste, sight, hearing, touch)
2. What types of words are used to appeal to the senses?
3. Though the author does not explicitly tell you anything about herself, what can you deduce about her lifestyle and interests? Give evidence from the text to support your comments.
4. What is the idea that the writer is trying to get across to her readers?
5. How does her use of description help to convey this idea?

Think about the following questions before you read the essay "Discus Thrower," by Richard Selzer.

1. Have you ever found yourself immediately liking or disliking someone based solely on their appearance?
2. When you sit down to eat a meal what are the very first clues as to whether or not you will enjoy the meal?
3. Have you ever heard a song that you immediately liked or disliked without really having heard the lyrics?

THE DISCUS THROWER

by Richard Selzer

1 I spy on my patients. Ought not a doctor to observe his patients by any means and from any stance, that he might the more fully assemble evidence? So I stand in the doorways of

hospital rooms and gaze. Oh, it is not all that furtive an act. Those in bed need only look up to discover me. But they never do.

2 From the doorway of Room 542 the man in the bed seems deeply tanned. Blue eyes and close-cropped white hair give him the appearance of vigor and good health. But I know that his skin is not brown from the sun. It is rusted, rather, in the last stage of containing the vile repose within. And the blue eyes are frosted, looking inward like the windows of a snowbound cottage. This man is blind. This man is also legless — the right leg missing from midthigh down, the left from just below the knee. It gives him the look of a bonsai, roots and branches pruned into the dwarfed facsimile of a great tree.

3 Propped on pillows, he cups his right thigh in both hands. Now and then he shakes his head as though acknowledging the intensity of his suffering. In all of this he makes no sound. Is he mute as well as blind?

4 The room in which he dwells is empty of all possessions — no get-well cards, small, private caches of food, day-old flowers, slippers, all the usual kickshaws of the sickroom. There is only the bed, a chair, a nightstand, and a tray on wheels that can be swung across his lap for meals.

5 "What time is it?" he asks.

6 "Three o'clock."

7 "Morning or afternoon?"

8 "Afternoon."

9 He is silent. There is nothing else he wants to know.

10 "How are you?" I say.

11 "Who is it?" he asks.

12 "It's the doctor. How do you feel?"

13 He does not answer right away.

14 "Feel?" he says.

15 "I hope you feel better," I say.

16 I press the button at the side of the bed.

17 "Down you go," I say.

18 "Yes, down," he says.

19 He falls back upon the bed awkwardly. His stumps, unweighted by legs and feet, rise in the air, presenting themselves. I unwrap the bandages from the stumps, and begin to cut away the black scabs and the dead, glazed fat with scissors and forceps. A shard of white bone comes loose. I pick it away. I wash the wound with disinfectant and redress the stumps. All this while, he does not speak. What is he thinking behind those lids that do not blink? Is he remembering a time when he was whole? Does he dream of feet? Of when his body was not a rotting log?

20 He lies solid and inert. In spite of everything, he remains impressive, as though he were a sailor standing athwart a slanting deck.

21 "Anything more I can do for you?" I ask.

22 For a long moment he is silent.

23 "Yes," he says at last and without the least irony. "You can bring me a pair of shoes."

24 In the corridor, the head nurse is waiting for me.

25 "We have to do something about him," she says. "Every morning he orders scrambled eggs for breakfast, and, instead of eating them, he picks up the plate and throws it against the wall."

26 "Throws his plate?"

27 "Nasty. That's what he is. No wonder his family doesn't come to visit. They probably can't stand him any more than we can."

28 She is waiting for me to do something.

29 "Well?"

30 "We'll see," I say.

31 The next morning I am waiting in the corridor when the kitchen delivers his breakfast. I watch the aide place the tray on the stand and swing it across his lap. She presses the button to raise the head of the bed. Then she leaves.

32 In time the man reaches to find the rim of the tray, then on to find the dome of the covered dish. He lifts off the cover and places it on the stand. He fingers across the plate until he probes the eggs. He lifts the plate in both hands, sets it on the palm of his right hand, centers it, balances it. He hefts it up and down slightly, getting the feel of it. Abruptly, he draws back his right arm as far as he can.

33 There is the crack of the plate breaking against the wall at the foot of his bed and the small wet sound of the scrambled eggs dropping to the floor.

34 And then he laughs. It is a sound you have never heard. It is something new under the sun. It could cure cancer.

35 Out in the corridor, the eyes of the head nurse narrow.

36 "Laughed, did he?"

37 She writes something down on her clipboard.

38 A second aide arrives, brings a second breakfast tray, puts it on the nightstand, out of his reach. She looks over at me shaking her head and making her mouth go. I see that we are to be accomplices.

39 "I've got to feed you," she says to the man.

40 "Oh, no you don't," the man says.

41 "Oh, yes I do," the aide says, "after the way you just did. Nurse says so."

42 "Get me my shoes," the man says.

43 "Here's oatmeal," the aide says. "Open." And she touches the spoon to his lower lip.

44 "I ordered scrambled eggs," says the man.

45 "That's right," the aide says.

46 I step forward.

47 "Is there anything I can do?" I say.

48 "Who are you?" the man asks.

49 In the evening I go once more to that ward to make my rounds. The head nurse reports to me that Room 542 is deceased. She has discovered this quite by accident, she says. No, there had been no sound. Nothing. It's a blessing, she says.

50 I go into his room, a spy looking for secrets. He is still there in his bed. His face is relaxed, grave, dignified. After a while, I turn to leave. My gaze sweeps the wall at the foot of the bed, and I see the place where it has been repeatedly washed, where the wall looks very clean and very white.

VOCABULARY AND COMPREHENSION

1. Selzer says that his spying, "is not all that furtive an act." What is the meaning of *furtive?* (par. 1)

2. The patient's skin is "in the last stage of containing the vile repose within." How does an understanding of the words *vile* and *repose* (par. 2) help the reader understand the seriousness of the patient's illness?

3. A **simile** which is introduced by "like" or "as" is a comparison of two essentially different things. Find an example of a simile in the second paragraph. What does it reveal about the patient's state of mind?

4. What is a *bonsai*? (par. 2) Explain the use of this particular word in reference to the patient.

5. Locate the word *deceased* in paragraph 49. Why does Selzer choose to use this word instead of the more direct, or harsh word *dead?*

6. Selzer uses the word *gaze* twice in the text: once in the first paragraph and again in the last paragraph. What is a gaze? How is the use of this particular word important to the meaning of the text?

ORAL DISCUSSION

1. a. Read aloud the three direct questions that Selzer asks his patient during the medical procedure.
   b. Do you believe that these three questions are perfunctory or half-hearted?

2. What is the author's attitude or tone throughout the story? Support your choice with evidence from the text.
3. Do you think the head nurse *approves* of the patient's behavior?
4. Do you think the doctor *approves* of the patient's behavior?
5. Reread the last paragraph of the essay. What "secrets" do you think the doctor is searching for when he returns to the room?
6. What is the significance of the title *The Discus Thrower*?

Do Not Go Gentle Into That Good Night

by Dylan Thomas

Do not go gentle into that good night,
Old age should burn and rave at close of day;
Rage, rage against the dying of the light.

Though wise men at their end know dark is right,
Because their words had forked no lightning they
Do not go gentle into that good night.

Good men, the last wave by, crying how bright
Their frail deeds might have danced in a green bay,
Rage, rage against the dying of the light.

Wild men who caught and sang the sun in flight,
And learn, too late, they grieved it on its way,
Do not go gentle into that good night.

Grave men, near death, who see with blinding sight
Blind eyes could blaze like meteors and be gay,
Rage, rage against the dying of the light.

And you, my father, there on the sad height,
Curse, bless, me now with your fierce tears, I pray.
Do not go gentle into that good night.
Rage, rage against the dying of the light.

ORAL DISCUSSION

1. Read the poem "Do Not Go Gentle Into That Good Night". To whom does the author Thomas address his poem and why?
2. Why do you think Thomas mentions four specific character types?

3. Would Thomas agree with the behavior exhibited by Selzer's patient? Why or why not?
4. Would Selzer agree with the advice offered by the speaker in Thomas' poem? Why or why not?
5. How do you think society views death?
6. Are the two writers' (Selzer and Thomas) attitudes and perspectives about death representative of attitudes in society in general? Explain your answer.

TOOLS OF THE TRADE

A Strong Introduction

In the same way that a good topic sentence *provides the focus* of a paragraph and *grabs the reader's attention,* a good **introduction** should *arouse the interest of the reader,* and *present the thesis or main point of an essay.* The reader's interest can be aroused by either a *brief anecdote,* a *description,* or *background information* concerning the topic. The main point or **thesis** is made clear to the reader through the use of a thesis statement.

A clear thesis statement is vital to a well-developed essay because it gives the writer a focus in writing and the reader a focus in reading the essay. The development of a thesis statement moves through several stages. First you have to think about the idea you want to write about. Next, you have to decide on a position to take on the idea. Once this is done, you have to word your thesis statement carefully. Be aware that everything you mention in your thesis must be discussed in your essay. Also, everything written in your essay must relate to your thesis statement.

Study the following example of the creation of a thesis statement.

IDEA: Companies are permitted by governments to cause pollution in order to increase profit.

POSITION: this is wrong

THESIS STATEMENT: While governments have previously turned a blind eye to companies that pollute in order to increase their profits, the current environmental crisis demands that the government take strong action to remedy the situation.

Look at the following sample introductions.

A

Although I do not believe in physical punishment, I think that many parents need to be more firm in the disciplining of their children. In the past, children were generally disciplined with an iron fist, and corporal punishment was the norm both at home and in the school. A wisecracking student would be flogged or strapped with a leather belt, and a child who talked back to his or her parent would usually get slapped for it. Indeed, an axiom of the past was that "children should be seen but not heard." Today, many parents have gone to the opposite extreme, and obnoxious behavior is not only accepted, but encouraged. It's not uncommon to hear, "Johnny is kicking me because he wants to get in touch with his feelings."

B

"I want it NOW! Buy it for me NOW! If you don't, I'll hate you forever!" `Randy' wanted a new video game, and he wouldn't take "no" for an answer. His mother begged him to quieten down, but Randy responded by shouting "BUY IT NOW, YOU WITCH!" The mother, in a moment of desperate fury, made an uncharacteristic gesture: she spanked her son. His screams and tears were now real. Feeling overcome with guilt, the mother quickly bought her son the video game. Scenes like this one occur throughout our country. Clearly, many parents need to be more firm and consistent in their disciplining methods.

1. Look again at the various introduction styles mentioned in this chapter. Introduction **A** is an example of which style?

____

2. Find the thesis statement in introduction **A** and write it in the space provided.

____

____

3. Introduction **B** is an example of which style?

____

4. Find the thesis statement in introduction **B** and write it in the space provided.

____

____

5. What conclusion can you make about where a thesis statement may be found in an introductory paragraph?

____

____

____

Read the body paragraphs and conclusion of this essay.

BODY 1

First of all, cats are much cleaner than dogs. When a cat needs to relieve itself, it does so with dignity. A small hole is dug in the dirt or the kitty litter, and the offensive material is neatly deposited there. Immediately afterwards, the cat covers up its "deposit" to ensure that the mess and the odour are hidden. Dogs leave their "mark" on any available lawn, and humans are expected to clean up the mess.

BODY 2

Moreover, cats are more cuddly than dogs. When people are feeling tired and lonely, cats are comforting with their soft, clean, silky fur and their reassuring purr. Dogs, on the other hand, with their odour, their awkward legs and their dripping tongues, are not my idea of a cosy pet.

BODY 3

Finally, cats are much easier and less expensive to care for than dogs. Cats can be left alone all day, and when their owners want to travel, their neighbors can easily take on the minor responsibility of leaving food for the cat. Dogs need to be walked every morning, every afternoon and every night; sometimes even in the middle of the night. Their owners have to invest in leashes and pooper scoopers in order to avoid paying hefty municipal fines. Dog owners who want to travel must either put their canines into an expensive kennel, or impose on very tolerant friends to care for their pets.

CONCLUSION

Clearly cats are a much better choice for a pet than dogs. In addition to being cleaner, more cuddly, and less expensive to care for than dogs, they are also more beautiful. Cats slink along with a dancer's ease, and their beautiful almond -shaped eyes are a joy to behold. When faced with the dilemma of cat or dog, choose the right one. Choose a cat!

WRITTEN EXERCISE

Write three different introductions for this essay. Use an anecdote, a description or background information to indicate your position and make sure that your thesis statement is clear.

WRITING CHALLENGE

Write a text in which you state your opinion on one of the following topics. Just as Richard Selzer did, include descriptive details to cntice your readers to think about your thesis.

1. Is life governed by fate?
2. Is there such a thing as an afterlife?
3. Do individuals enter the medical profession because they care about people?

The following question now has significance for you.
Add it to the **Writer's Tool Box** at the beginning of your book.

HAVE I WRITTEN AN EFFECTIVE INTRODUCTION WITH A CLEAR THESIS STATEMENT?

CHAPTER 4

Getting Your Message Across

Before you start this chapter, here are a few questions to consider:

* What methods do you use to convince your parents to see things your way?
* When you have discussions with friends, how do you get them to see your point of view?
* When you hear politicians speak, what methods do they use to sway public opinion?
* How would the level of language you might use to convince your parents or friends differ from the level of language a politician might use to convince his or her constituents?

PRE-READING

In this chapter you will be reading a complete opinion essay. Before doing so, read the following opinion paragraph and discuss the questions that follow.

MOSQUITO ARMIES

I am not a bug lover, generally, but I am willing to accept the "live and let live" principle. If a bug keeps a certain distance, I'm willing to forgo the urge to splatter it with a newspaper. No one can call me needlessly cruel. There is one tiny creature, however, that has set me to fantasizing about its extinction. Would the world be worse off without mosquitoes? Would birds still have enough to eat? Would anybody CARE if mosquitoes died off? Those long-nosed little pieces of wing are the bane of my existence. God knows our summers aren't THAT long, yet just when the winds of spring warm the air, just when the tiny flowers gingerly open their petals, just when it's not only easy, but pleasant to go for a long evening stroll, the mosquito armies arrive! They attack, they swarm, they chase, and they follow! In the moment that it takes to dart indoors, a few crafty mosquitoes always manage to sneak in with us. Then, in the dead of night, when we are busy dreaming of excellent adventures, a humming in our ear wakes us up. We turn on the light to hunt for the critter, but he manages to evade capture. He waits, patiently, for us to turn off the light, go back into our covers, forget about him, and doze off. Then, of course, he's baaacck. Back for our blood. Death to mosquitoes! May they all be bitten to death by a miniscule version of themselves!

ORAL EXERCISE

1. The author's thesis is that she does not like mosquitoes. What evidence is given to support this opinion?
2. Which arguments appeal to reason (facts) and which arguments appeal to emotion? How do you know when the argument is emotional or factual?
3. Why is it necessary for an author to use these two types of arguments?

THE FORMAL ESSAY

Two of the earlier essays, "Finishing School"and "The Discus Thrower" are written in an informal style. As you read these essays, you probably felt as though the authors were speaking directly to you. In addition to this, both authors made extensive use of the personal pronoun "I" throughout their work. This informal tone is one which you as a writer might adopt in informal writing such as friendly letters and personal reminiscences.

The next sample "HISstory" is much more formal in tone. The author has chosen to omit the personal pronoun "I". In addition, the vocabulary is more precise, the sentences more complex, and there is no use of dialogue. The formal essay is the type that is most likely to be required of you in academic writing.

HISSTORY

by Rene Taylor

1 At a recent educational colloquium, Annie Marcus, a well-respected educator, stated that every time she opens a history book she cringes. She is disappointed by literature anthologies; science books anger her. She went on to state that she hasn't always felt this way. She has discovered, after years of post-secondary education, that if a student is different in any way from other people, true knowledge can only come from self-education. This is especially true for any minority group, whether they be of another race, a different religion or, as in her case, of a different sexual orientation. After she had received all her *education* from public institutions, she started asking herself why there was no mention of gay people in the his-

tory books, why there were no gay writers, and why her biology texts never mentioned homosexuality as a part of the natural world. Was she the only gay person to have ever lived? Was she alone in the world? Then, through her own research, she discovered that there exists a slew of texts (not the ones that her teachers had assigned) that talk about the role gay men and women have played in history. It was at this time she realized that the very school system that was supposed to tell her about herself and her place in the world, had chosen to ignore her. Unfortunately, Marcus' experiences are not unique. The whole school system, and consequently its curriculum, is based on the fundamental assumption that all people are the same. This assumption is wrong. Not all people are the same. They differ in race, sex, religion and sexual-orientation, and if the school system wants to play its role in giving knowledge to all its students, it will have to embrace them all in its curriculum. Failure to teach gay students about themselves is irresponsible and results in grave consequences.

2 Traditional education has seen students as empty vessels waiting to absorb knowledge. This view of education makes students dependent on the teacher and relegates them to the role of being passive beings who depend on the teacher to tell them what to do and what things mean. As such, students' education is not theirs to create, appropriate, make over and shape. They are under the power of the teacher as an authority figure and are dependent on him or her for knowledge. This approach annuls learners' creative potential and deadens their critical faculties. As a result, knowledge is imposed on students, and teachers and school boards get to decide what that knowledge will be. As a result, the relationship between teachers and students is rarely harmonious because students view teachers as oppressors.

3 This teacher-student dynamic is especially unfortunate for gay students because they live in an uninclusive society whose very foundation is blatantly heterosexual and whose institutions have been built and maintained to foster and perpetuate this heterosexuality. In Canada, while groups that are oppressed on the basis of race, social class and sex are socially permitted and at least superficially encouraged (through governmental and social agencies as well as media rhetoric) to band together and fight against injustice, homosexuals are not even given this token inducement and, in fact, see that whenever there is a challenge launched against the status quo, there is very vocal and vehement opposition to it from large factions of society.

4 It is particularly difficult for gay students to thrive in the school system because they are part of an invisible minority. It is not usually possible, however, to accurately determine which students are homosexual or heterosexual based on any discerning physical or behavioral characteristics. Furthermore, the majority of students who are homosexual, regardless of their age, do not find the classroom a safe place to identify themselves as such.

5 For the homosexual student, knowledge about him/herself is determined externally. North American society, through its laws, religions and attitudes views homosexuality negatively. The gay student learns about these societal views either explicitly; through teachers' or peers' attitudes, religious laws or the media; or implicitly through exclusion of homosexuals or homosexuality from course materials and examples. The result is that the gay student learns that he or she is abnormal and unwanted and that his/her identity as a homosexual is determined by sexual behaviour. The heterosexual lifestyle, on the other hand, is legitimized in this same system since it is the accepted norm of the dominant societal structure. Schools perpetuate this dominant structure by developing the way students think about the world and act in it. Traditional education orients students to conform, to accept inequality, to accept their places in the status quo and to follow authority.

6 A consequence of this for gay students is that they both consciously and subconsciously internalize society's views of themselves. This, for the gay student, is of paramount importance. Gay students need to be given the information about their identities and realities which has been witheld from them in the past. For example, they are not taught in school that in other cultures gender is not defined as a male-female dichotomy. In the North American Indian culture, for instance, there are four gender categories: male, female, berdache and amazon.* Each of these four genders is embraced in that culture, not in relation to sexual behaviour, but as a separate spirit, each contributing something unique and valuable to the culture. Students also need to be told that homosexual behaviour is natural behaviour. There are countless examples in biological and anthropological literature of homosexual behaviour in non-human species. Students also need to be taught that throughout history, homosexual relationships have been both tolerated and accepted in many cultures throughout the world. Once gay students are exposed to this information, it will be possible for them to define their role in history and not accept the identity imposed upon them by society.

7 However, since homosexual students are not given this information, they are not allowed to see that they have a legitimate history and a true cultural identity separate from the one imposed upon them by society. Consequently, they adopt society's definition of themselves, and this leads to self-hatred which is manifested in abnormally high suicide rates, as well as behaviour (promiscuity and psychological maladjustment) that reflects the homosexual identity as imposed by the rest of society. This, in turn, is used by very vocal factions of society as support for their prejudiced views.

8 Now, Marcus is a teacher: a part of the very system that let her down. She made a conscious decision to join this profession because she realized that the only way to change the existing system was from within. Whenever she meets a new class of students for the first time, she spends a lot of time looking at students' faces. She wants to know her students as individuals; she wants to embrace their differences, and she wants them to become self-educators. She never wants one of her students to cringe when they open a book.

---

*In the North American Indian culture, there is a differentiation between the words sex and gender. This culture designates two sexes but four genders (the gender word *berdache* includes gay men and the word *amazon* includes gay women).

VOCABULARY AND COMPREHENSION

1. Why is it important to understand the meaning of the word *cringe* in the first sentence.

2. From context, what is the meaning of *slew* in the phrase "slew of texts"? (par. 1)

3. Explain the metaphor "empty vessels". (par. 2)

4. What does the author mean by "blatantly heterosexual"? (par. 3)

5. Does the word *thrive* in the expression "to thrive in the school system" have a negative or positive connotation? (par. 4)

ORAL DISCUSSION

1. What is the thesis of this essay?
2. What points does the author use to support the thesis?
3. Do you agree with the author's thesis? Why or why not?
4. The author concludes by saying that "the only way to change the existing system was from within." Do you believe that this tenet, or belief, is true only in the realm of education? Could this same principle be applied to other areas of society such as politics, health care and religion?
5. The tone of the introduction and conclusion is more personal and emotional than the supporting paragraphs. Why do you think the author chose to use this strategy?
6. In your opinion, is the author of this essay a male or a female?
7. Debate the following topic: Should reading material involving same-sex couples be allowed in all levels of the education system?

TOOLS OF THE TRADE

An Effective Conclusion

Below you will find the introduction to an essay. Read it and answer the question that follows.

> *I am in ecstasy! My body is not my own; it belongs to someone else. I am usually a person who likes to be in control of everything, but this feels so good that I don't care if I am never again permitted to control my body. My senses are alive; my body is radiating emotion and passion like never before. I feel as if I will never be the same after tonight. I was put on Earth to feel this way; I have found my destiny.*

1. Based on your reading of this introduction, what do you think this essay is about?

____

____

2. Now, read the conclusion to this essay.

> *While this may not be true for everyone, singing, for me is a truly religious experience. When I sing, it is as though my body is not actually producing the sound, but rather it is being used as a vessel for the sound to pass through. Each time this sound passes through my body, I am the most alive I have ever been. It is as though music has assumed a persona: I can taste its notes; I can smell its feeling: I can see its emotion; and I can hear its voice. When I sing, I am one with this universe— a universe that is pure, eternal, and beautiful.*

3. Having read the conclusion, state the topic of the essay.

____

____

4. In Chapter 3 you learned that an introduction is important in that it arouses the interest of the readers and usually gives them an idea about what the text will be about. In this essay, the introduction does not tell the reader what the text will be about, but it does something else. What is this "something else"?

____

____

When you write any text, you have a reason for writing it. You want the reader at some point to understand that reason. Your introduction will generally give the reader an idea of that reason. This reason will be developed and supported in the body of your essay. In order to tie the essay together, you need a conclusion. Here is a list of *do's and don'ts* that you should consider when developing your conclusion.

DO'S

1. Remind the reader of the thesis of the essay as well as its main points in a new and creative way. This can be done with an anecdote, a quotation, a **rhetorical question**, (a question asked for effect only) or a final comment.
2. Maintain the focus of the essay in your concluding remarks.

DON'TS

1. Don't merely repeat what has already been said.
2. Don't introduce new unrelated arguments or information in the conclusion.

3. Make sure that your conclusion is clear and concise. Remember you want to leave the reader with the final impression that *you* are convinced of what you have said.
4. Discuss or recommend a possible course of action for the reader.

3. Don't use words like *maybe*, *probably*, and *possibly* that leave the reader with the impression that you are uncertain of your opinion. Do not apologize!
4. Don't preach. Let the readers reach his or her own conclusions. If your arguments are convincing enough, you will have led the reader to understand your position. If you have any doubt, your arguments probably aren't strong enough and you should review the body paragraphs of your essay.

WRITTEN EXERCISE

Read the following personal essay. You will notice that there is no conclusion. Think about what you have learned about the role of an effective conclusion, and use this information to write one for this text.

THE THEORY OF SCHOOL RELATIVITY

My family recently decided to have a big reunion in Montreal. Aunts, uncles and cousins that I had not seen in ages were all gathered in a big hall for a full-day party that was, in my mother's eyes at least, the biggest social event in history. As everyone was shuffling into the hall we had rented for this monumental event, it was my job to greet everyone with a big, forced-sincere smile. " Hi aunt Sheila! How are you? I'm great! Oh, yeah, I'm still in school...no I haven't got a job yet...ha ha. " " Hi uncle Bruce! No, I'm not on the job market yet...ha ha...yeah, the easy life of a student!. " " Hi Grandpa...yeah, I'm still living off the government." By the end of the night I had been repeatedly harassed to the point where I now don't care if I ever see those people again. People from my parents' generation seem to be under the impression that being a student means living the easy life. Nothing could be further from the truth.

First of all, I don't just have one job; I have two. Being a student is full-time work. I wonder how many of my patronizing relatives would welcome twenty hours a week of classes followed by at least that much time spent doing homework. Is it possible that they have forgotten the stress and pressure that accompany studying for exams or frantically attempting to finish one of many papers that is due on the same day? I think that in their minds they don't see school as being work because students are not paid. To me, though, this only makes the student's job that much more thankless. While my narrow-minded relatives may not love their jobs, at least they are paid to do them. I, on the other hand, have to come up with money to support myself while I'm in school.

I not only have the job of studying but like most students, I also have to work at a menial part-time job. How would my relatives fare if they had to juggle two jobs? How would they feel if their evenings and weekends were spent flipping hamburgers or putting up with rude customers who complain because the sweater they want to buy isn't available in a fuchsia. Could they possibly imagine how it feels to have to put up with being treated this way for the privilege of being paid six dollars an hour? What's worse is that most students have to balance their employment and their school work. Employers are not known for giving students time off when they have exams at the end of the semester, and teachers seldom take into account the fact that most students have to work when they assign homework and plan tests. At the same time, it is probably these same adults who condescendingly ask their nieces and nephews when they are finally going to get a real job.

As if these two jobs weren't enough, most students have the added responsibility of trying to make connections and gain experience so that they might eventually have a chance of getting one of the ever-dwindling number of jobs in their field of study. Most of my relatives were my age at a time when jobs were plentiful and they were able to pick from numerous possibilities when they finished their education. I, however, have to spend a lot of time doing volunteer work in order to meet people who might offer me a job in the future.

WRITING CHALLENGE

Respond to one of the following statements by writing a formal essay. Make sure that your choice of vocabulary is precise and that you state your opinion clearly.

1. "HISstory" demonstrates that society shapes individuals through either culture and / or education. Do you agree with this statement?
2. Some philosophers, such as Aristotle, have stated that people under the age of thirty cannot be described as truly knowledgeable since they have not yet acquired sufficient experience. Do you agree with this theory?

The following question now has significance for you.
Add it to the **Writer's Tool Box** at the beginning of the book.

DOES MY ESSAY HAVE AN EFFECTIVE CONCLUSION?

CHAPTER 5

The Short Story

The essays you have studied so far have been based on the true-life experiences of the various authors. In the next few chapters you will be introduced to a different type of writing: the short story. Both these literary genres reflect the life experiences of their authors, but a short story is fiction, while an essay is non-fiction. Through short story writing, authors are free to create action (plot), people (characters) and place (setting) and even thesis (theme) to relate an experience to their readers.

The same way that an essay is organized into sections, (introduction, body and conclusion), a short story also has a certain structure. This structure is referred to as its **plot**. The plot is used to arrange all the action that takes place in the story. The **action** in any story can be one single event or a series of events, but usually this action arises out of some sort of **conflict** (a struggle between opposing forces). There are three different kinds of conflict:

* *character against character*: the main character may be pitted against one person or a group of people.
* *character against environment*: the main character may be in conflict with some external force (physical nature, society or fate).
* *character against him or herself*: the main character may have an internal emotional conflict.

The central character in this conflict is usually referred to as the **protagonist** (whether the character is likeable or not) and the "whatever" he or she is in conflict with is referred to as the **antagonist.**

ELEMENTS OF THE PLOT

1. The first part of the plot is called the **exposition**. This section introduces the characters, the situation and the time and place.
2. The second part, the **rising action**, usually introduces or complicates the conflict. The rising action requires an initiating incident that helps to propel the action forward. This is the moment when it is clear that there is a conflict in the story.
3. Next, there will usually be a **climax** or turning point to the story where all the conflicts and complications are resolved in some way.
4. Then, there is the **falling action**, where certain elements of the conflict are unraveled or made clear to the reader.
5. Finally, there is the **conclusion** where the situation that became unstable at the beginning of the story becomes stable again.

Based on the information you have just read about the plot of a short story, complete the following chart.

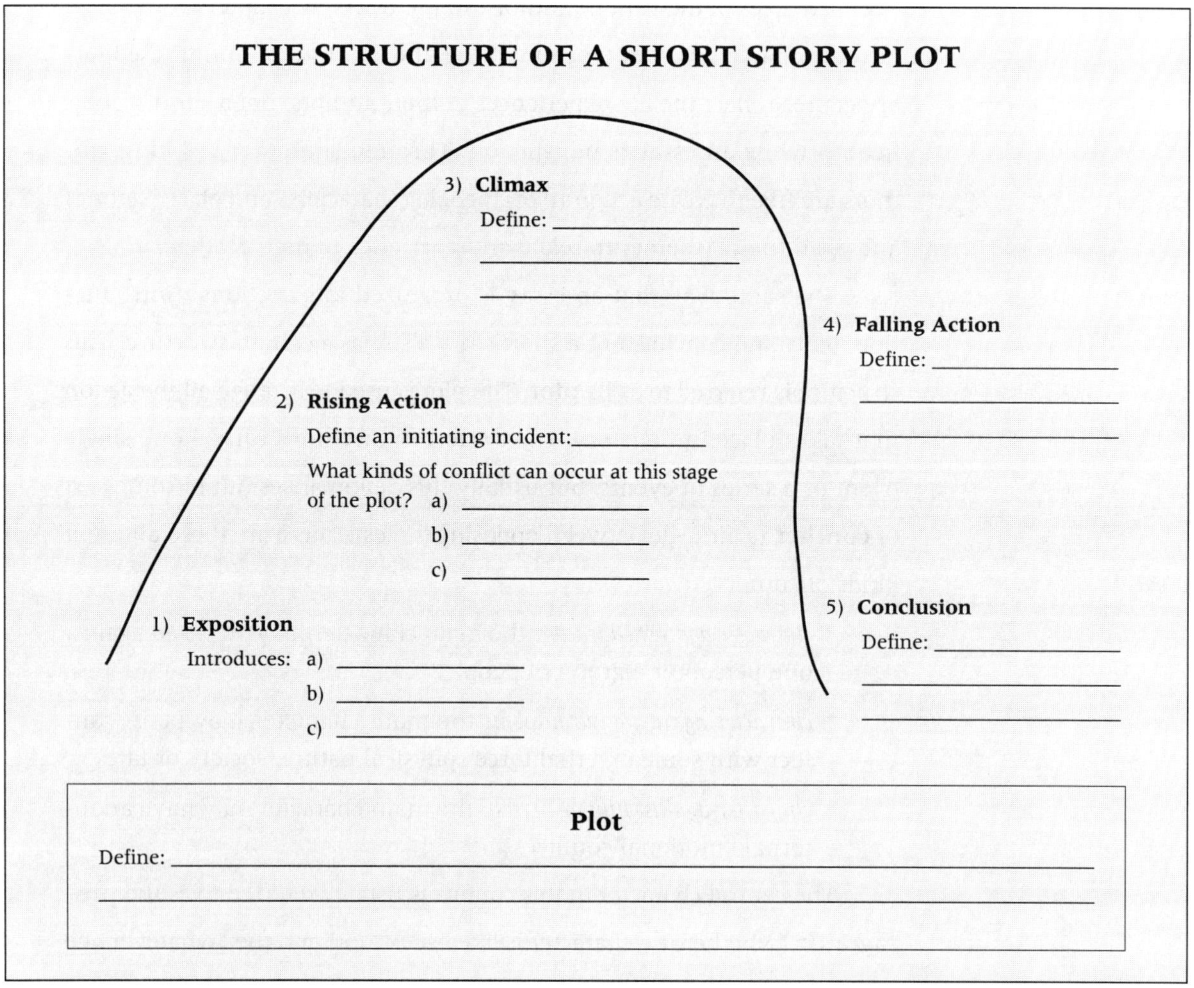

PRE-READING

Before you read the short story "Lamb to the Slaughter," by Roald Dahl, think about the following questions.

1. Do you think it is possible to get away with murder?
2. Are all people capable of murder?
3. When you think of murder mysteries you have read in the past, what has made them interesting?

Lamb To The Slaughter

by Roald Dahl

1 The room was warm and clean, the curtains drawn, the two table lamps alight — hers and the one by the empty chair opposite. On the sideboard behind her, two tall glasses, soda water, whisky. Fresh ice cubes in the Thermos bucket.

2 Mary Maloney was waiting for her husband to come home from work.

3 Now and again she would glance up at the clock, but without anxiety, merely to please herself with the thought that each minute gone by made it nearer the time when he would come. There was a slow smiling air about her, and about everything she did. The drop of the head as she bent over her sewing was curiously tranquil. Her skin — for this was her sixth month with child — had acquired a wonderful translucent quality, the mouth was soft, and the eyes, with their new placid look, seemed larger, darker than before.

4 When the clock said ten minutes to five, she began to listen, and a few moments later, punctually as always, she heard the tyres on the gravel outside, and the car door slamming, the footsteps passing the window, the key turning in the lock. She laid aside her sewing, stood up, and went forward to kiss him as he came in.

5 'Hullo, darling,' she said.

6 'Hullo,' he answered.

7 She took his coat and hung it in the closet. Then she walked over and made the drinks, a strongish one for him, a weak one for herself; and soon she was back again in her chair with the sewing, and he in the other, opposite, holding the tall glass with both his hands, rocking it so the ice cubes tinkled against the side.

8 For her, this was always a blissful time of day. She knew he didn't want to speak much until the first drink was finished, and she, on her side, was content to sit quietly, enjoying his company after the long hours alone in the house. She loved to luxuriate in the presence of this man, and to feel — almost as a sunbather feels the sun — that warm male glow that came out of him to her when they were alone together. She loved him for the way he sat loosely in a chair, for the way he came in a door, or moved slowly across the room with long strides. She loved the intent, far look in his eyes when they rested on her, the funny shape of the mouth, and especially the way he remained silent about his tiredness, sitting still with himself until the whisky had taken some of it away.

9 'Tired, darling?'

10 'Yes' he said. 'I'm tired.' And as he spoke, he did an unusual thing. He lifted his glass

and drained it in one swallow although there was still half of it, at least half of it, left. She wasn't really watching him but she knew what he had done because she heard the ice cubes falling back against the bottom of the empty glass when he lowered his arm. He paused a moment, leaning forward in the chair, then he got up and went slowly over to fetch himself another.

11 'I'll get it!' she cried, jumping up.

12 'Sit down,' he said.

13 When he came back, she noticed that the new drink was dark amber with the quantity of whisky in it.

14 'Darling, shall I get your slippers?'

15 'No.'

16 She watched him as he began to sip the dark yellow drink, and she could see little oily swirls in the liquid because it was so strong.

17 'I think it's a shame,' she said, 'that when a policeman gets to be as senior as you, they keep him walking about on his feet all day long.'

18 He didn't answer, so she bent her head again and went on with her sewing; but each time he lifted the drink to his lips, she heard the ice cubes clinking against the side of the glass.

19 'Darling,' she said. 'Would you like me to get you some cheese? I haven't made any supper because it's Thursday.'

20 'No,' he said.

21 'If you're too tired to eat out,' she went on, 'it's still not too late. There's plenty of meat and stuff in the freezer, and you can have it right away and not even move out of the chair.'

22 Her eyes waited on him for an answer, a smile, a little nod, but he made no sigh.

23 'Anyway,' she went on, 'I'll get you some cheese and crackers first.'

24 'I don't want it,' he said.

25 She moved uneasily in her chair, the large eyes still watching his face. 'But you *must* have supper. I can easily do it here. I'd like to do it. We can have lamb chops. Or pork. Anything you want. Everything's in the freezer.'

26 'Forget it,' he said.

27 'But, darling, you *must* eat! I'll fix it anyway, and then you can have it or not, as you like.'

28 She stood up and placed her sewing on the table by the lamp.

29 'Sit down,' he said. 'Just for a minute, sit down.'

30 It wasn't till then that she began to get frightened.

31 'Go on,' he said. 'Sit down.'

32 She lowered herself back slowly into the chair, watching him all the time with those large, bewildered eyes. He had finished the second drink and was staring down into the glass, frowning.

33 'Listen,' he said. 'I've got something to tell you.'

34 'What is it, darling? What's the matter?'

35 He had become absolutely motionless, and he kept his head down so that the light from the lamp beside him fell across the upper part of his face, leaving the chin and mouth in shadow. She noticed there was a little muscle moving near the corner of his left eye.

36 'This is going to be a bit of a shock to you, I'm afraid,' he said. 'But I've thought about it a good deal and I've decided the only thing to do is tell you right away. I hope you won't blame me too much.'

37 And he told her. It didn't take long, four or five minutes at most, and she sat very still through it all, watching him with a kind of dazed horror as he went further and further away from her with each word.

38 'So there it is,' he added. 'And I know it's kind of a bad time to be telling you, but there simply wasn't any other way. Of course I'll give you money and see you're looked after. But there needn't really be any fuss. I hope not anyway. It wouldn't be very good for my job.'

39 Her first instinct was not to believe any of it, to reject it all. It occurred to her that perhaps he hadn't even spoken, that she herself had imagined the whole thing. Maybe, if she went about her business and acted as though she hadn't been listening, then later, when she sort of woke up again, she might find none of it had ever happened.

40 'I'll get the supper,' she managed to whisper, and this time he didn't stop her.

41 When she walked across the room she couldn't feel her feet touching the floor. She couldn't feel anything at all — except a slight nausea and a desire to vomit. Everything was automatic now — down the stairs to the cellar, the light switch, the deep freeze, the hand inside the cabinet taking hold of the first object it met. She lifted it out, and looked at it. It was wrapped in paper, so she took off the paper and looked at it again.

42 A leg of lamb.

43 All right then, they would have lamb for supper. She carried it upstairs, holding the thin bone-end of it with both her hands, and as she went through the living-room, she saw him standing over by the window with his back to her, and she stopped.

44 'For God's sake,' he said, hearing her, but not turning round. 'Don't make supper for me. I'm going out.'

45 At that point, Mary Maloney simply walked up behind him and without any pause she swung the big frozen leg of lamb high in the air and brought it down as hard as she could on the back of his head.

46 She might just as well have hit him with a steel club.

47 She stepped back a pace, waiting, and the funny thing was that he remained standing there for at least four or five seconds, gently swaying. Then he crashed to the carpet.

48 The violence of the crash, the noise, the small table overturning, helped bring her out of the shock. She came out slowly, feeling cold and surprised, and she stood for a while blinking at the body, still holding the ridiculous piece of meat tight with both hands.

49 All right, she told herself. So I've killed him.

50 It was extraordinary, now, how clear her mind became all of a sudden. She began thinking very fast. As the wife of a detective, she knew quite well what the penalty would be. That was fine. It made no difference to her. In fact, it would be a relief. On the other hand, what about the child? What were the laws about murderers with unborn children? Did they kill them both — mother and child? Or did they wait until the tenth month? What did they do?

51 Mary Maloney didn't know. And she certainly wasn't prepared to take a chance.

52 She carried the meat into the kitchen, placed it in a pan, turned the oven on high, and shoved it inside. Then she washed her hands and ran upstairs to the bedroom. She sat down before the mirror, tidied her face, touched up her lips and face. She tried a smile. It came out rather peculiar. She tried again.

53 'Hullo Sam,' she said brightly, aloud.

54 The voice sounded peculiar too.

55 'I want some potatoes please, Sam. Yes, and I think a can of peas.'

56 That was better. Both the smile and the voice were coming out better now. She rehearsed it several times more. Then she ran downstairs, took her coat, went out the back door, down the garden, into the street.

57 It wasn't six o'clock yet and the lights were still on in the grocery shop.

58 'Hullo Sam,' she said brightly, smiling at the man behind the counter.

59 'Why, good evening, Mrs Maloney. How're *you*?'

60 'I want some potatoes please, Sam. Yes, and I think a can of peas.'

61 The man turned and reached up behind him on the shelf for the peas.

62 'Patrick's decided he's tired and doesn't want to eat out tonight,' she told him. 'We usually go out Thursdays, you know, and now he's caught me without any vegetables in the house.'

63 'Then how about meat, Mrs Maloney?'

64 'No, I've got meat, thanks. I got a nice leg of lamb, from the freezer.'

65 'Oh.'

66 'I don't much like cooking it frozen, Sam, but I'm taking a chance on it this time. You think it'll be all right?'

67 'Personally,' the grocer said, 'I don't believe it makes any difference. You want these Idaho potatoes?'

68 'Oh yes, that'll be fine. Two of those.'

69 'Anything else?' The grocer cocked his head on one side, looking at her pleasantly. 'How about afterwards? What you going to give him for afterwards?'

70 'Well — what would you suggest, Sam?'

71 The man glanced around his shop. 'How about a nice big slice of cheesecake? I know he likes that.'

72 'Perfect,' she said. 'He loves it.'

73 And when it was all wrapped and she had paid, she put on her brightest smile and said, 'Thank you, Sam. Good night.'

74 'Good night, Mrs Maloney. And thank *you*.'

75 And now, she told herself as she hurried back, all she was doing now, she was returning home to her husband and he was waiting for his supper; and she must cook it good, and make it as tasty as possible because the poor man was tired; and if, when she entered the house, she happened to find anything unusual, or tragic, or terrible, then naturally it would be a shock and she'd become frantic with grief and horror. Mind you, she wasn't *expecting* to find anything. She was just going home with the vegetables. Mrs Patrick Maloney going home with the vegetables on Thursday evening to cook supper for her husband.

76 That's the way, she told herself. Do everything right and natural. Keep things absolutely natural and there'll be no need for any acting at all.

77 Therefore, when she entered the kitchen by the back door, she was humming a little tune to herself and smiling.

78 'Patrick!' she called. 'How are you, darling?'

79 She put the parcel down on the table and went through into the living-room; and when she saw him lying there on the floor with his legs doubled up and one arm twisted back underneath his body, it really was rather a shock. All the old love and longing for him welled up inside her, and she ran over to him, knelt down beside him, and began to cry her heart out. It was easy. No acting was necessary.

80 A few minutes later she got up and went to the phone. She knew the number of the police station, and when the man at the other end answered, she cried to him, 'Quick! Come quick! Patrick's dead!'

81 'Who's speaking?'

82 'Mrs Maloney. Mrs Patrick Maloney.'

83 'You mean Patrick Maloney's dead?'

84 'I think so,' she sobbed. 'He's lying on the floor and I think he's dead.'

85 'Be right over,' the man said.

86 The car came very quickly, and when she opened the front door, two policemen walked in. She knew them both — she knew nearly all the men at that precinct — and she fell right into Jack Noonan's arms, weeping hysterically. He put her gently into a chair, then went over to join the other one, who was called O'Malley, kneeling by the body.

87 'Is he dead?' she cried.

88 'I'm afraid he is. What happened?'

89 Briefly, she told her story about going out to the grocer and coming back to find him on the floor. While she was talking, crying and talking, Noonan discovered a small patch of congealed blood on the dead man's head. He showed it to O'Malley who got up at once and hurried to the phone.

90 Soon, other men began to come into the house. First a doctor, then two detectives, one of whom she knew by name. Later, a police photographer arrived and took pictures, and a man who knew about fingerprints. There was a great deal of whispering and muttering beside the corpse, and the detectives kept asking her a lot of questions. But they always treated her kindly. She told her story again, this time right from the beginning, when Patrick had come in, and she was sewing, and he was tired, so tired he hadn't wanted to go out for supper. She told how she'd put the meat in the oven — 'it's there now, cooking' — and how she'd slipped out to the grocer for vegetables, and come back to find him lying on the floor.

91 'Which grocer?' one of the detectives asked.

92 She told him, and he turned and whispered something to the other detective who immediately went outside into the street.

93 In fifteen minutes he was back with a page of notes, and there was more whispering, and through her sobbing she heard a few of the whispered phrases — '... acted quite normal... very cheerful... wanted to give him a good supper... peas... cheesecake... impossible that she...'

94 After a while, the photographer and the doctor departed and two other men came in and took the corpse away on a stretcher. Then the fingerprint man went away. The two detectives remained, and so did the two policemen. They were exceptionally nice to her, and Jack Noonan asked if she wouldn't rather go somewhere else, to her sister's house perhaps, or to his own wife who would take care of her and put her up for the night.

95 No, she said. She didn't feel she could move even a yard at the moment. Would they mind awfully if she stayed just where she was until she felt better? She didn't feel too good at the moment, she really didn't.

96 Then hadn't she better lie down on the bed? Jack Noonan asked.

97 No, she said, she'd like to stay right where she was, in this chair. A little later perhaps, when she felt better, she would move.

98 So they left her there while they went about their business, searching the house.

Occasionally one of the detectives asked her another question. Sometimes Jack Noonan spoke to her gently as he passed by. Her husband, he told her, had been killed by a blow on the back of the head administered with a heavy blunt instrument, almost certainly a large piece of metal. They were looking for the weapon. The murderer may have taken it with him, but on the other hand he may've thrown it away or hidden it somewhere on the premises.

99 'It's the old story,' he said. 'Get the weapon, and you've got the man.'

100 Later, one of the detectives came up and sat beside her. Did she know, he asked, of anything in the house that could've been used as the weapon? Would she mind having a look around to see if anything was missing — a very big spanner, for example, or a heavy metal vase.

101 They didn't have any heavy metal vases, she said.

102 'Or a big spanner?'

103 She didn't think they had a big spanner. But there might be some things like that in the garage.

104 The search went on. She knew that there were other policemen in the garden all around the house. She could hear their footsteps on the gravel outside, and sometimes she saw the flash of a torch through a chink in the curtains. It began to get late, nearly nine she noticed by the clock on the mantel. The four men searching the rooms seemed to be growing weary, a trifle exasperated.

105 'Jack,' she said, the next time Sergeant Noonan went by. 'Would you mind giving me a drink?'

106 'Sure I'll give you a drink. You mean this whisky?'

107 'Yes, please. But just a small one. It might make me feel better.'

108 He handed her the glass.

109 'Why don't you have one yourself,' she said. 'You must be awfully tired. Please do. You've been very good to me.'

110 'Well,' he answered. 'It's not strictly allowed, but I might take just a drop to keep me going.'

111 One by one the others came in and were persuaded to take a little nip of whisky. They stood around rather awkwardly with the drinks in their hands, uncomfortable in her presence, trying to say consoling things to her. Sergeant Noonan wandered into the kitchen, came out quickly and said, 'Look, Mrs Maloney. You know that oven of yours is still on, and the meat still inside.'

112 'Oh, *dear* me!' she cried. 'So it is!'

113 'I better turn it off for you, hadn't I?'

114 'Will you do that, Jack. Thank you so much.'

115 When the sergeant returned the second time, she looked at him with her large, dark, tearful eyes. 'Jack Noonan,' she said.

116 'Yes?'

117 'Would you do me a small favour — you and these others?'

118 'We can try, Mrs Maloney.'

119 'Well,' she said. 'Here you all are, and good friends of dear Patrick's too, and helping to catch the man who killed him. You must be terrible hungry by now because it's long past your supper time, and I know Patrick would never forgive me, God bless his soul, if I allowed you to remain in his house without offering you decent hospitality. Why don't you eat up that lamb that's in the oven? It'll be cooked just right by now.'

120 'Wouldn't dream of it,' Sergeant Noonan said.

121 'Please,' she begged. 'Please eat it. Personally I couldn't touch a thing, certainly not what's been in the house when he was here. But it's all right for you. It'd be a favour to me if you'd eat it up. Then you can go on with your work again afterwards.'

122 There was a good deal of hesitating among the four policemen, but they were clearly hungry, and in the end they were persuaded to go into the kitchen and help themselves. The woman stayed where she was, listening to them through the open door, and she could hear them speaking among themselves, their voices thick and sloppy because their mouths were full of meat.

123 'Have some more, Charlie?'

124 'No. Better not finish it.'

125 'She *wants* us to finish it. She said so. Be doing her a favour.'

126 'Okay then. Give me some more.'

127 'That's the hell of a big club the guy must've used to hit poor Patrick,' one of them was saying. 'The doc says his skull was smashed all to pieces just like from a sledge-hammer.'

128 'That's why it ought to be easy to find.'

129 'Exactly what I say.'

130 'Whoever done it, they're not going to be carrying a thing like that around with them longer than they need.'

131 One of them belched.

132 'Personally, I think it's right here on the premises.'

133 'Probably right under our very noses. What you think, Jack?'

134 And in the other room Mary Maloney began to giggle.

VOCABULARY AND COMPREHENSION

1. How does the title *Lamb to the Slaughter* foreshadow, or give a clue about, the outcome of the story?

2. Does the spelling of *tyres* for *tires* (par.4) seem strange ? What does this spelling tell you about the geographical setting of this particular story? What does the use of this form tell you about language in general?

3. Mary Maloney found her pre-dinner drink with her husband "blissful" (par. 8). Furthermore, it is indicated that Mary "loved to luxuriate in the presence of this man." "Her eyes waited on him for an answer, a smile, a little nod, but he made no sign." (par.22) What do these phrases tell you about Mary's personality and her relationship with her husband?

4. In paragraph 50, Mary asks herself a series of questions after having killed her husband. What do these questions tell you about another aspect of her personality?

____

____

5. In the Grammar Appendix, sentence fragments are discussed. The line, "A leg of lamb." (par.42) is an obvious fragment. Why does this line stand alone? Why do you think Roald Dahl chose to use a fragment?

____

____

6. How is Dahl playing a word game when he writes that Detective Noonan discovers *congealed* blood on the head of the victim (par.89)? HINT! Look for possible meanings for the word congealed.

____

____

7. Using the chart at the beginning of this chapter, answer the following:

Exposition

a) Where does the story take place?

____

b) Who is the protagonist?

____

Who is the antagonist?

____

c) Describe the situation in the first part of the story.

____

____

____

Rising Action:

a) What is the initiating incident that moves the story forward?

____

b) What is the conflict (or conflicts) in the story?

____

____

Climax

What part of the story could be described as the climax or turning point?

____

____

____

Falling Action

What is the falling action in the story?

____

____

____

Conclusion

How does the story conclude?

____

____

____

ORAL ACTIVITIES

1. One group of students will assume the role of defense counsel for Mary Maloney. Another group will assume the role of the prosecution. Each side must prepare to present the facts to convince a jury of her innocence or guilt.

2. You are a member of the jury. You have heard all the facts. Determine whether Mary Maloney is guilty of murder or not guilty by reason of insanity.

TOOLS OF THE TRADE

Planning an Essay

You have probably seen a house under construction at one time or another. You have also realized that the construction would be costly and disorganized without adequate planning and carefully created blueprints. The same principle is true when writing an essay. Adequate planning of your essay will allow for easy writing and solid effective results.

You have learned in previous chapters how to plan a paragraph. You are now going to see how planning an essay requires that you use what you have already learned in relation to the paragraph and that you build upon this knowledge.

STRUCTURE OF THE ESSAY

INTRODUCTORY PARAGRAPH

Sentence 1 – Arouse the reader's interest.

Give background, description or narration.

Thesis statement – State your position clearly.

THE BODY OF THE ESSAY

Body Paragraph 1

Sentence 1 – Arouse the reader's interest. Link this paragraph to the previous paragraph by using a transitional word or phrase.

Support arguments – Each of these must relate to sentence 1.

Concluding point – Refer back to sentence 1, but do not repeat.

Body Paragraph 2

Sentence 1 – Arouse the reader's interest. Link this paragraph to the previous paragraph by using a transitional word or phrase.

Support arguments – Each of these must relate to sentence 1.

Concluding point – Refer back to sentence 1, but do not repeat.

Body Paragraph 3

Sentence 1 – Arouse the reader's interest. Link this paragraph with the previous paragraph by using a transitional word or phrase.

Support arguments – Each of these must relate to sentence 1.

Concluding point – Refer back to sentence 1, but do not repeat.

CONCLUDING PARAGRAPH

Sentence 1 – Arouse the reader's attention and let the reader know that you are about to conclude.

Link this paragraph with the previous paragraph by using a transitional word or expression.

Restate the main ideas in the three body paragraphs.

Finally do one of the following: make a recommendation, suggestion or prediction.

TRANSITIONAL WORDS

When developing an essay, you want to assure that the reader's journey through your arguments is smooth and uninterrupted. **Transitional words** help you to achieve smooth sentence and paragraph flow. Without these words and phrases, your essay risks appearing disjointed.

The following is a list of the most common transitional words. Insert them as needed in your own writing.

Common Transitional Words

next	besides	then	however	thus
consequently	furthermore	indeed	in addition	therefore
moreover	hence	nevertheless	on the contrary	as a result
whereas	although	even though	in spite of	similarly

WRITING CHALLENGE

Create a plan for an essay using the chart above to help you. Then write a formal essay in which you respond to one of the following statements.

1. If Mary Maloney had been a man and the victim a woman, the police would have been less accommodating and more suspicious.
2. Everyone has the capacity to commit evil acts.
3. You can only push people so far before they snap.

The following question now has significance for you.
Add it to the **Writer's Tool Box** at the beginning of your book.

DID I PLAN MY ESSAY BEFORE BEGINNING TO WRITE?

CHAPTER 6

Character Development

When you are getting to know people you have just met, you learn about them in various ways. Some of the clues you use to form an impression about people are as follows:

* how they look
* how they act
* what they say and how they say it
* what others say about them

When authors write, they want the reader to form a relationship with the characters they write about. In just the same way that you use clues in real life, authors will give the reader clues to help make their characters come to life. Authors reveal character through a combination of methods:

* direct description of the character
* the character's actions
* the character's dialogue
* what they say to and about each other

Since you, as a reader, are forming a relationship with the characters in a story, your personality as well as your interpretation of the characters will influence the type of relationship you have with the characters. For example, in the last story you read, "Lamb to the Slaughter," by Roald Dahl, it is possible to argue that the protagonist, Mary Maloney, was either a diabolical, calculated murderess, or simply a woman that has been pushed too far. A good author gives only clues about character and challenges the readers to reach their own conclusions.

PRE-READING

1. Can you think about any relatives you have who could be described as a little quirky or idiosyncratic?
2. Have you ever noticed any peculiar behavior at family gatherings?

MONKEY ON MY BACK

by Paul L. Vasey

1 Our duffel bags hadn't even hit the floor when Aunt Ruth staggered from the kitchen.

2 "Mabel's in the bug-house!" she proclaimed before collapsing into her nagahyde E-Zee chair, cradling her highball like a newborn child.

3 "I gotta git this munkey off my back," she muttered.

4 "JESUS CAA-RYST Ruth, would you shut-up! The Price is Right's on!" Uncle Fred bellowed.

5 Aunt Ruth's head rolled from shoulder to shoulder, as if possessed by a demon. "Ferrred! Ferrred!... Mabel's in the bug-house!" she screeched in a painfully nasal voice, "I just gotta git this munkey off my back!"

6 The news about Aunt Mabel's incarceration came as no surprise to my brother, Todd, and me. We had been repeatedly warned by our mother about "Dad's common-as-dirt relatives and their crazy, backwoods antics." My mother never had a kind word for these relatives. In her mind she had saved my father from damnation when she married him and insisted they move as far away from his family as possible. Since Mom insisted on avoiding contact with them as much as possible, Todd and I had only met our relatives a couple of times in our lives. Dad, on the other hand, never said anything about his family and whenever we asked questions about them, he would just change the subject.

7 We had not told my mother that our trip to Ontario would include a quick visit back to the town of Crinklewood and the bosom of our extended family. We had to see for ourselves what Mom had been warning us about for years. Like gawking spectators at a circus freak-show, we gravitated to them; simultaneously repelled and fascinated by their white-trash, rough-trade lifestyles. Like anthropologists in deepest, darkest Africa, we wanted to scrutinize, dissect and discuss their every move in detail. For Todd and I, a visit with our extended family was as exciting and exotic as travelling to a Moroccan Casabah or the Brazilian Mardi Gras.

8 "I'll be turnin' over in my grave before I spring your DUNNKOFF of a sister out of the LOONIE-BIN! They should lock up every GAWD-DAMNED one of ya up and throw away the key! HAHAHAHA!"

9 Bob Barker's voice blasted from the TV reminding viewers to *"spade and neuter your pets."*

10 This latest family crisis was nothing new. Death, insanity, divorce, financial collapse, and rare and debilitating diseases were all part and parcel of the "antics" our Mom had warned us about. She had stated emphatically on many occasions that Dad's kith and kin were

her constant reminder that Darwin had only gotten it half right. While my relatives had obviously made it down from the trees, their very existence signaled the end of evolution; a complete breakdown in the laws governing the universe.

11 Once, my Aunt Anna had lost her life savings in a chain-letter get-rich-quick-scheme that made her go on a mad stampede, destroying the second floor of my grandmother's house and screaming over and over "I'm a maniac... I'm a maniac....". Another time, my cousin, Dell, contracted neurofibromatostic macacafuscata, a little known disease carried by mosquitoes and common only to those inhabiting the lower Ren-Si Valley in Laos. No one had any idea where the hell that mosquito had come from, but Uncle Stan swore it was "one of those GAWD-DAM COMMUNISTS that brought it into *our* country." After this, Uncle Stan began wearing mosquito-mesh undergarments.

12 "You kids want dinnah?" Aunt Ruth asked.

13 "Ferrred! Make us some burgers, Ferrred, before I come over there and THUMP yaa," she cajoled.

14 In his nagahyde E-Zee chair, Uncle Fred gripped his stomach and said in mock-laughter, "JESUS CAA-RYST Ruth, if you so much as laid one mitt on me, I'd knock you all the way to the moon ... KAABOOOM!"

15 The TV flickered with a Michelin Tire commercial. The company's trademark, a big, fat, white humanoid-thing that looked like a million marshmallows all blobbed together, danced across the screen.

16 "Hi Fred! Hi Fred! Hi Fred!" Aunt Ruth called out to the dancing TV character.

17 "I'm gonna hafta come over there and WHOMP yaa Ruth" Uncle Fred warned, raising his hand for emphasis.

18 "HAHAHA!! Yaa can't take the heat, can yaa Ferred" she replied. Then waving to the marshmallowy blob she cackled over and over "Hi Fred!... Hi Fred!... HAHAHA!!".

II

19 During dinner my brother and I managed to piece together the story. Apparently, Aunt Mabel had been committed to the local mental hospital following a drunken, midnight rampage in which she had slugged two care-workers and a security guard at her retirement home. As her legal guardian, my Aunt Ruth was called in by the authorities to rectify matters. This entailed a trip to the psych ward and various meetings with the medical staff, signing the appropriate paperwork, and, worst of all, getting custody of my Aunt Mabel.

20 "You kids understand don't cha? I just gotta git this munkey off my back!" she appealed to us, raising her umpteenth highball of the day to her lips.

21 The ever present commentary from the TV droned on and on. *In a surprise drug-bust early this morning O.P.P. officers raided an infamous crack house in the Jane and Finch area of Metro-Toronto. Crack is a synthetic form of cocaine, but is cheaper and five times more addictive. Members of the special police drug-task force estimate that the amount of crack seized has a total street value of $60 million. Nine individuals were arrested at the time of the raid, four of them minors. Police report more arrests are pending, as are further raids. CTVO News will keep you, the viewer, posted on any other crack-related stories which unfold in the coming days as police continue their get tough policy on the fight against drugs in our city.*

22 Aunt Ruth's eyes narrowed on my brother and I. "You kids don't take drugs do you?"

23 "Well," my brother responded, "heroin — but only for medicinal purposes," and then laughed.

24 The ice-cubes in Aunt Ruth's scotch and water tinkled as she raised the glass to her mouth, regarding my brother suspiciously.

25 "He's only joking, Aunt Ruth," I assured her, but this didn't seem to work. Aunt Ruth looked as though she was now mulling over the possibility she was harboring crack addicts; maybe we were even contemplating operating a crack *network* right from her very living room.

26 "Ruth!" my Uncle barked out as he lathered Heinz mustard onto his burger, "these buns ain't Wonderbread!"

27 "Nah, there the E-TALIAN kind Ferred."

28 "GAWD-DAM SHIT!" my uncle replied.

29 "Wadda-yaa say we take these boys to that Chinese restaurant in Crestwood tomarrow night fer dinnah?" Never one to wait for a response to his questions, Uncle Fred turned to us and said "Best GAWD-DAM CHINESE food yaa ever laid a lip over!"

30 "Wadid I have there the last time Ferrred? Sweet and sour chicken balls! They were DE-lish-E-ous!"

31 "Tommarrow nite we'll git ourselves a feed of that Chinese food! HEEHEEHEE-HAA!"

32 As if to emphasize the culinary epiphany that awaited my brother and I, both my aunt and uncle licked their lips and simultaneously hummed "MMMMMMMMMM!!!!"

33 The TV rambled on, "... a rare species, the Chinese golden monkey, will be the latest addition to the family at the Metro-Toronto Zoo. Only one other colony of this primate exists outside of..." Eyes transfixed on the TV screen, the smile melted from my Aunt's face as she reached for her drink.

34 "I gotta get this munkey off my back," she muttered.

III

35 The drive to Crestwood took about forty-five minutes, and all the way we were promised "the best GAWD-DAM CHINESE food this side of TOKEEYO." My Uncle beeped the car horn at every other pedestrian we passed, tossing off a cheery wave to the confused person and laughing uproariously. Aunt Ruth had been drinking steadily since breakfast and by now was engaged in a garbled conversation with herself, "... I dunno... PHUTTT... I dunno .... PHUTTT... I dunno ... PHUTTT...." she repeated over and over like a broken record. She wore a fur hat of unknown origin but it looked to me like it had come from a mutant wolverine that had undergone extensive radiation therapy. With the hat skewing wildly to one side of her head, she looked like she had just crawled out of a ditch.

36 Not surprisingly, dinner was less than spectacular. Small town Ontario is not noted as a center with flair for international cuisine. The typically uninspired North American version of Chinese food was offered up: deep fried chicken balls, sweet and sour shrimp, fried rice, limp chow mein. Nonetheless, Todd and I were on our best behaviour and gushed about the wonderfully authentic meal, but I secretly wondered whether I was eating stray cat.

37 On the way out, the hostess handed us each a little almond cookie. It was in the shape of a monkey. Aunt Ruth suddenly looked ill, but managed to ask "What's this?"

38 "Year of the monkey" the hostess replied, patting her on the back and smiling.

IV

39 I didn't feel so well the next morning when I awoke to the TV commentary. *Another crack ring was busted late last night in the Metro-Toronto area of Gerrard and Parliament. This is the second largest drug bust by O.P.P. police in the past week and they vow to break the back of the crack network in our city. Thirteen individuals were arrested. Police representatives declined comment citing their concerns over jeopardizing future operations against crack houses that are in the works... In other news, the Metro-Toronto zoo's new golden monkeys....*

40 "Are you *sure* you kids don't take drugs," Aunt Ruth persisted as she refilled the ice-cube trays.

41 "No" we replied shaking our head.

42 "GAWD-DAM drug-addicts!" my Uncle ranted, "They should ship 'em all up to Baffin Island and shoot 'em along with all them people involved with communism, atheism, and faggenism!"

43 While Aunt Ruth was guzzling in the kitchen and Uncle Fred was busily scanning TV game shows like a speed reader, I slid over to Todd on the sofa.

44 "Do you feel sick?" I asked.

45 "Yes," he replied, "the pains in my stomach are killing me."

46 "Me too." Suddenly, we both realized what had happened. "Oh my God," I whispered, "food poisoning from the Chinese food!"

47 "GAWD-DAM Wheel of Fourchun," Uncle Fred cursed, "too many Americans on it!.... There's one from the sun-shine state!... How yaa doin' sunshine... HAHAHAHA!!!"

48 "PHUTT... PHUTT... I dunno... I dunno... PHUTT," drifted out from the kitchen.

49 "What are we going to do?" Todd asked.

50 "You kids come in here," Aunt Ruth hollered.

51 "Just act normal," I told Todd, "the last thing we need is to upset Aunt Ruth even more by telling her we were poisoned at her restaurant of choice." I ground my teeth from the pain and hauled myself into the kitchen. Todd followed.

52 We both squeezed into the small space. Aunt Ruth was sprawled on a folding chair, leaning heavily on the kitchen card-table. Arms stretched straight out in front of her, she clutched her scotch as if in prayer. Pulling herself up, she tried to convey some semblance of control over current events and said "Now you kids know that Mabel's in the bug-house...and it's mee they're callin ta git 'er out... yer granmuther don't want nothin' ta do with it... " As if to fortify herself she took another belt of her scotch. "Now, you kids gotta help me with this mess... this afternoon Ferreds drivin us ta the bug-house ta git 'er out and you kids is gonna help mee... I mean... I dunno... I dunno... PHUTT!!"

53 "GAWD-DAM DUNNKOFF!" Uncle Fred yelled at one of the hapless game show contestants, "yaa wouldn't know yer ass from page nine!"

54 "What exactly is it that you want us to do, Aunt Ruth?" my brother asked. I bit my lip to keep from wincing from my stomach pains.

55 She pointed her finger at us. "You two gotta talk to them doctors and see whether we're gonna leave 'er in the bug-house or not." Todd and I exchanged pained glances.

56 "I gotta git this munkey off my back," she said reaching for her bottle of Johnny Walker Red. "... PHUTT...."

V

57 That afternoon at the mental hospital we were lead into a large room full of patients.

58 "This place is filled with more FRUITS and NUTS than a LAURY SECORD CHRISTMAS CAKE!" Uncle Fred yelled at the top of his lungs. Suddenly, Aunt Mabel materialized out of the woodwork and came swooping towards me. She gripped my shoulders like a bird of prey and harpy-shrieked into my face "YOU GOTTA GIT ME OUWDA HERE!!!".

59 So much for teary family reunions.

60 It had been years since I had last seen Aunt Mabel, but, like a figure from Madame Toussaud's wax museum, she hadn't changed and, in fact, she really did seem thoroughly waxen. She had always had this crazy "What Ever Happened to Baby Jane" quality that made me think that she was either going to break out into some drunken vaudevillian song and dance or else clobber me.

61 "Now Mrs. Shaw. Please calm yourself," a weary looking nurse pleaded. "Mrs. Ruth Wagner?" the haggard nurse queried.

62 No answer. Aunt Ruth was transfixed, staring at Aunt Mabel who was ranting at Uncle Fred.

63 "Mrs. Ruth Wagner?" the nurse tried again.

64 "It took yaa GAWD-DAM long enough ta git here," Aunt Mabel screamed at Aunt Ruth.

65 "Mrs. Wagner?" the nurse pleaded, touching Aunt Ruth's shoulder.

66 I could see Aunt Ruth marshaling all her inner strength to put on as composed a facade as possible. Like a businesswoman taking charge of a corporate meeting, she poised herself and replied authoritatively, "Yes, I'm Ruth Wagner, Mabel's younger sister."

67 "Yaa can re-sight the family lineage layter Ruth, NOW GIT ME THE HELL OUTTA HERE!"

68 "Now Mrs. Shaw. Don't speak to your sister like that. She's come to help you dear," the nurse interjected softly.

69 *"She's come ta help yaa deeeaaar,"* Aunt Mabel mimicked, making faces at the nurse. "Move it Ruth! There's papers upstairs ya gotta sign," she ordered, pushing Aunt Ruth towards the elevator.

70 "Now Mrs. Shaw, aren't we getting a little ahead of ourselves, dear? Your sister will have to talk to the doctor before any papers can be signed."

71 "I KNOW THAT," Aunt Mabel hollered at the nurse, her face turning puffy and red "AN' IF YA CALL ME DEAR ONE MORE TIME I'LL KNOCK YER HEAD OFF, DEAR! Why don'tcha run along an' give somebody a sponge bath!"

72 Right about then, one of the other hospital residents wandered up to the bedraggled nurse. "Have ya had a poke today?" he asked with one of those Cheshire Cat smiles that only the truly insane are capable of.

73 Aunt Mabel buckled over with fits of laughter, "Ya give it ta 'er honey," she yelled, slapping her new-found friend on the back.

74 The poor nurse had not counted on the likes of my Aunt Mabel. After this latest attack on her dignity, her face turned to stone. She turned to my Aunt Ruth and said "Room 549, Fifth Floor" then walked away briskly mumbling under her breath "Hillbilly White Trash!" Uncle Fred fled to the safety of the car.

75 "MOVE IT RUTH!...We ain't got all day... yer gonna make me miss Jeopardy!"

76 Aunt Mabel herded us all into the elevator like cattle going to the slaughter. At this

point my stomach pains began to take on a whole other dimension. This was not just mere pain, no sir, this was somewhat akin to being repeatedly stabbed in the stomach with a dull shovel. I could see our act of *bonne santé* starting to crumble. My brother looked like he was losing his mind.

77 Out of nowhere he looked into space and queried, "where's the price-tag machine?" taking out his wallet and turning it over and over again. My eyes widened in horror. "Oh no, not now! Don't flip out on me here!" I thought, but there was little I could do since merely standing upright was difficult at that point.

78 "WHAT!" Aunt Ruth spat out "Whadid yaa say?... the *PRICE-TAG MACHINE*??? Wadda ya talkin' about? What in the HELL is wrong with you KIDS? Are yaa taking CRACK!" Todd just kept turning over his wallet again and again, apparently looking for the elusive price-tag machine. Aunt Mabel seemed oblivious to all this, preoccupied with the thought of missing this afternoon's episode of Jeopardy.

79 I tried ineptly to cover up for Todd. "It's nothing Aunt Ruth," I said nervously, "he's just playing a game... like... I SPY... ya... I SPY... PRICE TAG MACHINE!... HAHAHAHA... That's a hard one, Todd!... HAHA."

80 Then it hit me... a wave of pain, like an earthquake, and my gut formed the epicenter. I doubled over; water welling up in my eyes. I grabbed my stomach and cried out "OH MY GODDD!!!" Needless to say, my little outburst did nothing to improve Aunt Ruth's confidence in our past history of drug use.

81 "He's goin' through CRACK with-drawal!!!" she screamed.

82 "WE'RE HERE!!" Aunt Mabel cried out as the elevator doors opened. "Now try an' act normal far CHRIST SAKE!!!"

83 Aunt Ruth was insistent. "NOW WAIT-A-MINIT!!! Where have you two been keepin' the CRACK, I wanna know!!!"

84 "I don't know, I only come here for breakfast," Todd politely replied to no one in particular, his eyes glazed over like a gecko.

85 "It's part of the game... I SPY... get it, Aunt Ruth?... I SPY?" It was no use. Aunt Ruth would not sway; we were crack addicts period and probably running a drug ring too.

86 Aunt Mabel paraded us down the hall to Room 549. Not waiting to knock, she flung open the door and walked into the doctor's office. We all filed in looking embarrassed and the doctor just stared at our motley crew with his mouth agape: me, half-mad with pain, rubbing my stomach; Todd searching for the price-tag machine; Aunt Ruth half-drunk with that mutant-wolverine-hat falling down over her eyes; and Aunt Mabel half-crazy, but certainly more in control of the situation than the rest of us.

87 "I *adore* Belgian chocolates," Todd babbled to the confused doctor while I whimpered in the corner.

88 "PHUTTT!" Aunt Ruth intoned, shaking her head.

VI

89 By the following evening things seemed to have calmed down. Aunt Mabel had been released from the mental hospital and our bout of food poisoning appeared to have lifted, but unfortunately we hadn't managed to convince Aunt Ruth that we weren't crack addicts. Explaining that we had been poisoned by the Chinese food just seemed out of the question; anyhow, she would never have believed it.

90 That night my Aunt Anna put on a big party to celebrate Aunt Mabel's return to the world of mental health.

91 "Oh my God!" Todd exclaimed as we pulled up to the dilapidated farmhouse Aunt Anna called home. The clapboard monstrosity leaned dangerously to one side, like an old shed which had endured the ravages of too many storms. Brown paint peeled off the warped boards and laid curled up on the porch like abandoned moth pupae. The place was choking in acres of flotsam; wrecked automobiles, oven doors, dismantled ski-doos, rusty refrigerators, unwound coils of barbed wire fencing and mountains of tires. Clucking chickens ran hither and thither and white eggs were visible amongst all the junk, where clumps of raspberry bramble and rhubarb battled each other for oxygen. Broken glass, firewood, and discarded gun cartridges were scattered about liberally. Like many other small Ontario towns, times had not been good to Crinklewood. The town's economy had long since collapsed when Crinklewood's main employer, the Ding Dong Maraschino Cherry factory, moved south to Mexico. With the departure of the Ding Dong factory an aimlessness overtook Crinklewoodians which seemed to be reflected in the helter skelter of my Aunt Anna's home.

92 "Com'on in an' have a piece a cheesecake!" Aunt Anna hollered from the junk strewn porch. Some gooey batter dripped off a wooden spoon, which she had just used to scratch her enormous behind. So immense, in fact, was my Aunt's *derriere*, that my mother was fond of commenting how a dinner plate could comfortably be placed on top of it, with space to spare for a wine glass, a napkin and salt and pepper shakers. This assessment lead to my brother, Todd, and I to christen Aunt Anna: "Table-for-one." Her big grin showed off a mouth full of rotten teeth: all yellowy-brown and gnarled like weathered tree stumps, with holes so big, one half-expected a squirrel to poke its head out of one of them. She was dressed in a worn cotton moo-moo that spread out like a Ringling Brothers tent to just below her knees, where vericose veins crawled like vines of ivy away from a 49 cent pair of flip-flops topped with plastic blue daisies.

93 Inside her home, all my relatives milled about. The sight of them shocked me to my very core. It was like the Addams Family assembled for Halloween. My cousin Barabra-Ann was sitting on the floor with one leg hooked over her head. Dressed in hot pink spandex, she struggled to raise her other leg and farted. Barbara-Ann was a stripper. Word had it that she performed a simultaneous strip tease with her pet monkey, Woo, under the billing "FAMILY THIGHS." Woo, would come on stage dressed in drag — a veritable simian transvestite — and then he would strip down to his panties as Barbara-Ann did her thing. To me it sounded like some sort of twisted musical revue combining all the elements of Swank magazine and Mutual of Omaha's Wild Kingdom.

94 Tonight, Woo sat high atop the curtain rod, eyeing me, shamelessly attired like a Southern Belle in a frilly peach-colored frock. My brother swore that Woo was evidence for some early stage in the evolution of cross-dressing.

95 Aunt Anna had already broken out the cheesecake, serving up heaping hunks of it on flimsy paper plates.

96 "It's SARY LEE, don't ya know?" she informed us, beaming with pride.

97 "Did ya hear their lett'in those COMMUNIST monkeys into *our* country?" Uncle Stan asked anyone who would listen. "Gotta be careful."

98 "Careful about what?" I asked myself. The likelihood that an endangered species of

Chinese monkey posed a serious threat to Canadian national security did *not* strike me as a pressing concern. After I politely declined his offer to make me a pair of mosquito mesh underpants, he scooped up a piece of cheesecake and shoveled it into his mouth.

99 As the evening wore on, the alcohol began to take its toll and the whole atmosphere became more and more surreal. Everyone's behavior took on a larger than life quality as if they were living out a cinematic pairing of "Deliverance" and "Another World". A cacophony of curses ensued.

100 Aunt Ruth was menacing Uncle Fred from one end of the kitchen table with a steel meat mallet. "Ya ain't NEVER gonna git any a my GAWD-DAM money Ferred!"

101 "Ya can shuve the friggin turkey up yer ass!!!" Aunt Anna barked at Uncle Stan at the other end of the kitchen for some unknown deed he had committed.

102 Aunt Mabel gyrated lewdly on the coffee table holding up her vodka and tonic and singing out "MAMA'S COOKIN' NOW! MAMA'S COOKIN' NOW!"

103 Barbara-Ann suddenly tore through the kitchen at break-neck speed carrying a rifle. She burst out the back door nearly ripping it off its hinges and ran across the yard sending sod flying in every direction. In the confusion, Woo jumped down from his perch, removed his panties and started flinging Aunt Ruth's cheesecake about the room.

104 "BERSERK!" Barbara-Ann screamed as she raced off into the woods.

105 "What an understatement," I thought. And then it hit me. At that moment I understood what my mother could never possibly understand and what my father, in his silence, understood all too well. In the same way that the television filled their otherwise empty days, their antics provided them with the distraction of some much needed drama. In a town where nothing ever happened they *deserved* their little melodramas, they had *earned* them. They kept life bearable.

106 It seemed like a good time to slip out since my brother and I had overstayed our welcome anyway. In her alcoholic haze, Aunt Ruth had threatened to call the police and report us as drug addicts and crack dealers. She had already torn apart every inch of her house looking for our "stash" and Uncle Fred kept interrogating us about our "Colombian connection."

107 We quietly made our getaway that evening and caught the next bus out of town; after all, with Aunt Mabel taken care of, the last thing Aunt Ruth needed was another monkey on her back.

VOCABULARY AND COMPREHENSION

Since authors use words to develop their characters, it is important that they choose their words carefully. In the story, "Monkey on My Back," there are many words that are used to give you clues about various characters. Consider the choice of words as you answer the following questions.

1. How does the mother's reference to the relatives' *antics* (par. 6) help the reader to discern her feelings about the relatives?

____

2. The narrator's mother, "had stated emphatically on many occasions that Dad's *kith and kin* were her constant reminder that *Darwin* had only gotten it half right." (par. 10)

   Is the use of *kith* and *kin* sarcastic? What does its use tell the reader about the mother?

   ____

3. What does the reference to *Darwin* mean? What does it reveal about the mother? (par. 10)

   ____

   ____

4. What does the fact that Ruth *staggers, (par. 1) cradles her highball,* (par. 2) and *clutches her scotch as if in prayer* (par. 52) tell you about Ruth's relationship with alcohol?

   ____

   ____

5. What does the use of the word *screeched* tell you about the quality of Ruth's voice? (par. 5)

   ____

6. What aspects of Fred's character are revealed by the fact that he *ranted (par. 42)* and *cursed*. (par. 47)

   ____

7. The narrator says that Uncle Fred, "beeped the horn at every other pedestrian we passed, *tossing off a cheery wave* to the confused person and *laughing uproariously*." (par. 35)

   What clue does this give you about another dimension of Uncle Fred's personality?

   ____

   ____

8. "Apparently, Aunt Mabel had been committed to the local mental institution following a drunken, midnight rampage in which she had *slugged* two care-workers..." (par. 19)

   Why do you think the author chose to use the word *slugged* instead of *hit*?

   ____

9. Why is it important to understand the reference, or allusion to, *harpy-shrieked* in order to complete the image of Mabel *swooping* (par. 58) when the narrator visits her in the mental institution?

   ____

   ____

10. The narrator states, " Like anthropologists in deepest, darkest Africa, we wanted to *scrutinize, dissect* and *discuss* their every move in detail." (par. 7) What does this tell us about his initial motivation for visiting the relatives? Is the narrator more like his mother or his relatives and why?

____

____

ORAL DISCUSSION

1. What is the significance of the title *Monkey on My Back* in relation to the plot of the story?
2. Why would the author choose to include voices coming from the television throughout this story?
3. The family's dialogue is quite different from that of the author and his brother. How does this help to extend the comparison of their family visit to anthropologists exploring a new and strange culture?
4. What *epiphany*, or realization, does the author experience at the end of the story? How would the mood of the story be different without this epiphany?
5. To what degree are the sentiments expressed in the story universal for all families? Use examples from the story to support your answer.

TOOLS OF THE TRADE

Defining Character

A thorough definition of character can require examination of the **physiology**, **psychology** and **sociology** of that character.

Physiology	***Psychology***	***Sociology***
sex	morals	socioeconomic class
age	ambitions	occupation
height / weight / shape	frustrations	education
color hair/ eyes/ complexion	temperament	home life
posture	religion	complexes
general appearance	race	(superiority / inferiority,
physical handicaps	amusements	extrovert / introvert)
heredity	community status	abilities
		IQ

Though you may not be able to discern every element of character listed here, it is your job as a critical reader to find all support the author gives when describing a character, and evaluate how well the characters are developed.

Think about the various family members described in "Monkey on My Back". Imagine what the author's family photo album would look like. Since you, as a reader, do not have the benefit of pictures, the only way you can create a picture of his family is through a careful examination of the author's word choice. If a writer has done a good job in developing his or her characters, this should be easy to do. A clear **word-picture** will be created.

WRITTEN EXERCISE

In small groups, choose one of the following characters and create a word-picture: the narrator, Mom, Aunt Ruth, Uncle Fred or Aunt Mabel. Base your word-picture on direct descriptions of the characters, the characters' actions, what the characters say and how they say it, and what the characters say about each other. Be sure to include physiological, psychological and sociological elements.

WORD-PICTURE

Physiological	*Psychological*	*Sociological*
________________	________________	________________
Evidence:	Evidence:	Evidence:
________________	________________	________________
________________	________________	________________
________________	________________	________________
Evidence:	Evidence:	Evidence:
________________	________________	________________
________________	________________	________________
________________	________________	________________
Evidence:	Evidence:	Evidence:
________________	________________	________________
________________	________________	________________

* Is the character **dynamic** (undergoes change during the story) or **static** (remains the same)?

Give reasons to support your answers.

ORAL EXERCISE

Point of view is the perspective from which a story is told. Authors can approach a story from an *all-knowing,* third person point of view (**omniscient**) with themselves as the narrator of the story. An omniscient narrator knows everything that goes on in the minds of the characters. On other occasions, such as in "Monkey on My Back," the narrator is also a character in the story. In this case, the narrator's point of view is *limited* because he or she is confined to reporting only what can be seen, smelled, heard, tasted, and touched.

Look again at the scene when the narrator and his Aunt and uncle are in the Chinese restaurant. Role play the scene and vocalize the thoughts of one of the following characters:

* Aunt Ruth
* Uncle Fred
* a waitress in the restaurant

TOOLS OF THE TRADE

Analyzing Character

As a reader, you undoubtedly have opinions about what you read. Some works please; others do not. Whatever the case, when you make a value judgement of this sort, you are engaged in **literary analysis**. The same elements authors use to write a story (plot, character, setting and theme) are discussed in literary analysis to make an assessment about the strengths and weaknesses of a particular work. As with any written discourse, there are certain guidelines for writing a formal literary analysis.

An essential part of literary analysis is a character analysis. A character analysis is not simply a description or list of a character's attributes. It is a discussion of how these attributes are used to enrich and develop the story as a whole. For example, in "Lamb to the Slaughter," there is almost no description or development of Mary's husband, even though he is the antagonist. It is not important whether he is tall or short, Catholic or Protestant, intelligent or not; the author reveals only enough to show us that the husband is the antagonist and provides the initial conflict that propels the action forward. This was probably done to focus the reader's attention on the protagonist (Mary) since it is the complexity of her character and her actions that make the story more compelling.

Stylistically, a short story analysis is always written in the present tense. Since a literary analysis is considered academic writing, you should avoid using personal pronouns such as *I, me, you, we* and *us*.

A SEQUENCE FOR CHARACTER ANALYSIS

1. Gather information about the physiological, psychological and sociological aspects of the characters.
2. Ask yourself the following questions:
   - Who are the main characters (protagonist, antagonist)?
     What role do they play in the development of the plot?
   - How well are the characters developed?
     Are the characters true to life?
     Are the characters static or dynamic?
     Are the characters interesting?

In the short story, "Monkey on My Back," for example, the conflicts that occur are a direct result of the characters' personalities. Therefore in this story it is imperative that the author fully develop his characters.

WRITING CHALLENGE

Using the **TOOLS OF THE TRADE** discussed above, plan and write a character analysis of a character from "Monkey on My Back." Do not forget to support your analysis with evidence from the text.

The following question now has significance for you.
Add it to the **Writer's Tool Box** at the beginning of your book.

HAVE I INCLUDED A CHARACTER ANALYSIS AS PART OF MY SHORT STORY ANALYSIS?

CHAPTER 7

Setting

All stories are part of their time, place and culture. The setting of the story helps the reader to more fully understand the details of the story. Sometimes the setting is simply the location in which the action takes place. At other times, the setting itself is as important as the characters, the action and the theme because it provides the story with an environment that allows certain conflicts to emerge and it helps to justify the characters' motivations.

For example, in the short story "Monkey On My Back," the fact that the Ding Dong Maraschino Cherry Factory closed, influenced the lives of the characters. It could be argued that Uncle Fred sat at home all day and Aunt Ruth took to the bottle because of the prevailing economic difficulties. Therefore the time (*after an economic upheaval*), the place (*Crinklewood*) and the culture (*social status of Aunt Ruth and company*) had a direct effect on the development of the story.

PRE-READING

1. Have you ever wished you were someone else?
2. Do you believe you are a product of your environment?
3. Do your material possessions define what or who you are?

Gold Wings

by Leo McKay Jr.

1 I remember the first time I saw Paul Semple's father's motorcycle. It was a Sunday late in the summer that I turned fifteen. A week later, I saw the motorcycle again. Something terrible happened in the space of those seven days. Terrible.

2 On the last night of summer, the night before the first day of school, Kevin McPhadden and I were hanging out on *Ford Street,* the main street in town. We leaned back against the glass storefront of Superior Fuels, watching the cars go by. We stood and sat on the concrete steps for hours, from early in the afternoon until the sun had almost set. We'd sit down and watch the cars go by, spitting down between our feet onto the sidewalk. When our feet went to sleep, we'd stand up, shake out our legs, and use the height we'd gained to spit clear across the sidewalk, over the curb, and onto the street. Cars passed slowly, full of people we didn't know. Now and then a car pulled into the Quik Pik across from us and the driver got out. We'd watch through the big front window as the driver wandered around inside the store, eventually getting back into the car and driving off.

3 By the time the shadow of Stedman's department store had passed across the street, eclipsing the sun, Kevin and I had darkened a wide slice of sidewalk and a small half-moon of road pavement with our spit. The sky was the dark, cold blue of a summer emptied of heat. Clouds trickled past overhead like water in a slow stream.

4 As I thought about returning to school the next day, I remembered having left school in June — the way I'd felt. I remembered leaving class and going out the front door into the schoolyard with an armload of dog-eared notebooks. I had walked to the far side of the yard to a garbage can at the edge of the basketball court. I pushed back the lid of the can, letting it swing back and forth a couple of times while I hoisted the notebooks to my shoulder. Then I jammed the stack of scribblers into the garbage. I sighed, dusted my hands, and went home. The whole summer had lain ahead of me.

5 "Maybe I won't go back," Kevin said suddenly. He looked away from me as he said it. He looked down the street to the south. He spat another dot onto the sidewalk.

6 "Home?" I said. A car with no muffler sped past, leaving a long cloud of blue smoke hanging over the street.

7 "What?" Kevin said. He looked at me.

8 "Go back where?" I said. "Home?" I knew a few things about Kevin's life at home, and I would not have blamed him if he didn't want to go back there. I knew, for instance, that Kevin had seventeen brothers and sisters, and that most of them lived at least part of the time at home. They lived in a Red Row house, an old mining company house exactly like mine. At Kevin's place, twenty people shared the same amount of space I often complained was too small for my parents, my kid brother, and me.

9 Out behind the McPhadden house were two early seventies model Chev Impalas, big wide boats of cars. The only thing wrong with these cars was that they didn't run. They had seized up from disuse. Each night from mid-May to October, a red and black wool blanket wrapped about him, Kevin made his bed in one or the other of the cars. "It's lonely out there," he told me one day. "But I like it. Nice soft seats to sleep on, radio. Too crowded in-

doors anyways." When the night was clear he slept in the faded blue Impala, because the battery was not yet dead, and he could listen to CKEC Radio in New Glasgow. When it rained he slept in the dark blue, because the windows rolled up tighter.

10 Kevin narrowed his eyes, thinking about what I'd asked. "Not go back home," he said. "That's not a bad idea." He shook his head and looked back up the street. "School," he said. "Shit."

11 "School," I said. "What would you do?"

12 He turned back to look at me. He had a long, thin scar that ran from under his hairline to the corner of one eyebrow. The way the light had started to dim made the scar stand out white. "Anything," he said. "I'd do anything."

13 Across the street Paul Semple, a guy my age, came out of an alley and went through the front door of the Quik Pik.

14 "Not that asshole," Kevin said. We watched as Semple passed up and down the narrow aisles of the Quik Pik.

15 "He's not so bad," I said. "He's all right."

16 "You can't believe a word that guy says," Kevin said.

17 "So," I said. "I don't. I don't believe a word."

18 There is a name for people like Paul Semple, people who make things up. I knew the name even when I was fifteen. I'd learned it from a magazine article I'd read: pathological liar. Although he lived in Valley Woods, "The Country's Premier Subdivision," as the sign assured the people who lived there, Paul never seemed satisfied with his life as it really was. Given the chance, he would exaggerate any story out of shape, or else he'd make a new story up fresh, right off the top of his head.

19 Paul came out of the Quik Pik sucking on a bottle of pop. He stood on the sidewalk, looked up at us, and smiled.

20 "Oh, Jesus," Kevin said.

21 Paul loped in long strides to our side of the street. "Jesus, Jesus," Kevin said.

22 "Shut up," I said. I elbowed Kevin.

23 "Hey, boys," Paul said when he reached us. He smiled in a silly way and bobbed his head up and down. "Not home sharpening up those pencils?"

24 "Already got them sharpened," I said. I held out my hand.

25 He put the bottle in my palm. Spitting all afternoon had dried my mouth. I took a long drink.

26 When I lowered the bottle, Paul took it back and said, "You want some?" He looked into the space between Kevin and me. Kevin twitched his head toward his shoulder.

27 Paul balanced on his toes on the edge of the concrete step and kept the silly smile on his face. He rocked back and forth and started talking. He had a loud, strong voice and he liked to use it. He talked about the school year that was about to begin. He told us that he already knew what homeroom he'd be in because he'd broken into the school and fished the information out of a filing cabinet in the principal's office.

28 "Bullshit," Kevin said. He started kicking the ground with his feet.

29 I elbowed him. I knew the story was a lie as well as he did, but I didn't see any point in contradicting it. Paul would only insist all the more that it was true.

30 "Care to place a bet?" Paul challenged. He held his hand out to Kevin and looked

into his face. "There's a photocopy of the class list on the desk in my bedroom. I can show you anytime. I can also tell you what class *you're* in, McPhadden, if you care to know."

31 Kevin was getting edgy, eager to take Paul up on his bet. I put myself firmly between the two of them and said: "We'll all find out tomorrow. I'd hate to spoil the surprise." Then I started laughing, and even though it was a fake laugh, it seemed to take the edge off the situation. Kevin settled down a little. His feet stopped shuffling against the ground.

32 Paul stood down from the edge of the step. He relaxed a little and slouched against the side of the door frame we were standing in. It wasn't long before he was talking about the motorcycle his father had bought the day before. It was a Gold Wing, he said. A seven-fifty. It had chrome this and chrome that. He said his father had bought it from an ex-Hell's Angel who was now selling bikes in Halifax.

33 We listened to Paul go on about the bike for a few minutes, neither of us saying much. Then Kevin said, "How's your old man getting this bike home from Halifax?"

34 "He took it back in a truck he borrowed from work," Paul said.

35 "Already here is it?"

36 "Yes. It is."

37 "In town?"

38 "Yes."

39 "I suppose your old man is out for a nice long ride on a day like today."

40 "He's working today. He works Sundays," Paul said.

41 "I see. Took the bike to work, did he? Wants to show it off to his friends?"

42 "He doesn't want to leave it in the parking lot for eight hours," Paul said. "It isn't safe."

43 "Sure," Kevin said. "It isn't safe."

44 "It's not," Paul said. Then, looking only at me, he said: "You want to see it?"

45 "Sure," I said.

46 Paul looked at Kevin. "You coming too?" he asked half-heartedly.

47 Kevin knew that a lot of parents didn't like their kids hanging around with him. Some of his brothers had been in jail, and the McPhadden name was not a good one to have in town. He would usually save a kid the embarrassment of bringing him home — and himself the embarrassment of not being invited — by refusing outright to visit anyone's house.

48 "I'm going," Kevin said. "You bet I am."

49 Valley Woods was the kind of neighbourhood the Brady Bunch lived in. I had seen Valley Woods plenty of times before, but always from the back end: picnic tables, clotheslines, lawn mowers, jungle gyms. There was a path that led from the elementary school in town, through a stand of woods, to a small clearing on a hill. Beyond this clearing the path continued through a gully, across a brook, and into Valley Woods itself, but I had never taken the path that far. On the weekends during the summer a gang of us would take the path to the clearing, where we'd sit on fallen trees and drink beer. After dark you'd see lights come on in people's kitchens, a passing outline of someone's head. That day, though, with Paul leading the way, we entered Valley Woods from the front end. We saw carports and hedges, wrought iron railings, paved driveways.

50 My father had always told me I was a Canadian but that all the places I saw on TV were American. I guess as a kid the differences you see are the obvious ones. But as we walked past the low, modern houses of Valley Woods, I was in America. At the other end

of town, in the Red Row, the neighbourhood Kevin and I lived in, the houses were tall and old and pointed, company houses from the mining days. Sure, I had been in rich neighbourhoods around the county before. Maybe it would be Christmas and my family would be looking at the lights. But the world looks different from inside a car. It's a lot like TV, seeing things pass by on the other side of that windshield. When you walk, you move slowly. You see things. I remember wondering what Kevin was thinking as we walked into Valley Woods.

51 It stood gleaming in the driveway, the proof of its own existence. Paul ran ahead so he could sit on it while we watched. Kevin was right behind me, and I heard him let out the smallest sound at the sight of it. Neither Kevin nor I knew anything about bikes, and neither of us spoke as Paul went through the same description he had given us on the main street. We didn't need it now. Words only cheapened the glory we felt in standing next to such a machine. The gas tank and a small triangular cover plate on each side were silken, unblemished red. The last rays of light from the sky glinted off the chrome. Paul settled onto the seat and crouched down, as though to slice through wind.

52 "Let me sit on it," I said.

53 Paul got up. I sat on the seat and twisted the throttle. I made a motorcycle noise. I leaned forward and looked up over the handlebars and across the backyard. I thought of power, and of going places.

54 "You'll flood it," Paul said.

55 "Sorry," I said. I let go of the throttle and sat up straight. "Cool bike," I said.

56 "You want to sit on it?" Paul asked, looking straight at Kevin.

57 Kevin was staring at his shoes. "You sick?" he said. He made a move toward the street with his head. "You coming?" he asked me.

58 I looked at Paul.

59 He shrugged.

60 "Yeah, sure," I said. "I guess I should be getting home." I got off the bike.

61 Paul stood in the driveway as we left. When we reached the road I looked back and noticed his mother in the front window, looking out at Kevin and me. She met Paul at the door as he went in.

62 It was a week later, on Sunday, that Paul Semple phoned me. It was dusk, and when the phone rang I was standing at the screen door at the back of our house, watching the sun set over the hills to the west of town.

63 I heard my mother get up from the couch in the living room and go into the kitchen. "Hello," she said. Then she called my name.

64 "You seen Kevin today?" Paul wanted to know.

65 "No. I haven't seen him since..." I thought for a moment. "Wednesday." He hadn't been in school Thursday or Friday.

66 "We went to his house, but he wasn't there," Paul said. "We asked his mother when she'd seen him last, but all she said was, 'A while ago.'"

67 Someone had stolen the dream machine. The Semples had gone to bed the night before, and when they woke up it was gone. There wasn't much the police could do. They interviewed the neighbours, but nobody had seen or heard anything.

68 At supper time, the Campbells, the Semples's nextdoor neighbours, arrived home from a day at the beach. Mrs. Campbell worked the four to twelve shift at the Michelin plant in Granton. She told Paul's father she'd been coming home from work at about one in the morning when she'd seen Kevin walking up the street in the direction of the Semple house. She'd thought at the time to phone the police, she said. But she remembered having seen Kevin in the Semples's driveway the week before.

69 "What are you saying?" I asked Paul.

70 "We're not saying anything," Paul said.

71 "I don't think he knows how to drive a bike," I said.

72 "Dad says even if he didn't take it, maybe he saw who did."

73 "Aw, cripes," I said. I felt my heart sink to a place deep inside me.

74 I hung up the phone. My mother was sitting at the table with a cup of tea. "What's wrong?" she asked.

75 "Nothing," I said. I took a banana from the top of the fridge and sat down across from her. As I ate I thought about Kevin. On the way home from Valley Woods the week before, that bike was all I'd talked about. How cool it was. How fast it would go. Kevin had told me to shut up about it.

76 I threw the empty peel into the garbage can by the stove and walked outside for the first time that day. My mother called after me to put on a jacket.

77 People hadn't closed the curtains on their front windows yet, and as I walked from the Red Row to Valley Woods, I looked shamelessly in at them as they sat in front of their televisions. Fat, middle-aged men and women and their kids. The blue light from the TVs made them look as if they'd come from a planet unknown to me. Kids not much younger than I was were already in pyjamas, watching the end of *The Wonderful World of Disney*. Women stood over sinks, washing supper dishes. Men watched the last football game of the weekend. By the time I reached Valley Woods the light was gone from the sky. Night had fallen completely. The curtains were closed in the windows of the houses I passed.

78 There was movement behind the curtains of the Semple house. The floodlight over the driveway seemed a memorial to the lost motorcycle. I stood only a moment. I was conscious that I was from the Red Row, and people would be on the lookout, now that something had gone wrong.

79 I walked up the street and turned down a footpath I thought must be the one that led north to the clearing where my friends and I drank. Kids from Valley Woods used the path every day through the week, but on the weekends their parents told them to stay away from it. They'd heard the teenagers drinking there.

80 The path was dark, but the moon was coming up through the trees in the east. The smell is what I noticed, the smell of trees and earth. The ground was springy beneath my feet. I smelled the needles of pine and spruce.

81 A swath of stars, fading as the moonlight increased, dipped through the trees overhead. I followed the path downhill to a place where it turned sharply to the left and crossed a brook. At the top of the rise on the other side of the brook would be the clearing. Alder bushes grew at the bottom of the gully. I reached the mossy bank of the brook and stopped, putting my weight on my front foot to jump to the opposite side. Standing poised to jump, with my arms out from my sides for balance, I took in a breath. There was a strange smell

in the air. A dull, metallic smell, stronger than the smell of nature. Gasoline.

82 I peered into the woods on either side of the path I was following. Something looked strange back where I'd turned, something I hadn't noticed when I'd gone past. White flesh of broken alder branches showed against the black shadows of leaves.

83 I went back to the bend in the path and looked straight into the woods, straight where you'd go if you didn't turn when the path did. The alder branches were broken and pushed away where something had gone through. I saw a glint of chrome in the moonlight.

84 The bike lay on its side in the brook. The water wasn't deep enough to cover it, but its gas tank was half-submerged. Moonlight reflected off a blue gasoline rainbow on the water's surface. A scorch mark blackened the chrome below the gas tank, where a little fire had burned, then gone out.

85 I jumped across the water to the opposite bank. Kevin lay face down at the base of a thick spruce. His arms were at his sides deliberately, the way a fifteen-year-old boy will hold his arms while he stands on someone's doorstep after walking her home from the dance. He doesn't want to stand too close to her. She might get angry. And he doesn't yet know what to do with hands.

86 He shifts his weight from one foot to the other. He makes a silly joke. She laughs nervously. Inside him are the sharp spikes of terror, but he knows that all he must do is ride out this moment. In the end she will stand quietly and look at him. He will take one step toward her, and their lips will briefly meet. On the way home, he will smile like a man drunk on oxygen, stumbling over cracks in the sidewalk.

87 Kevin lay there stiffly, forever determined to inhabit the same moment in time. On the rough bark of the spruce, a few feet above his head, there was a mark, a smudge, a smear of red lipstick.

VOCABULARY AND COMPREHENSION

1. Explain the narrator's attitude about school conveyed in the lines, "Then I jammed the stack of scribblers into the garbage. I sighed, dusted my hands and went home." (par. 4)

2. An ironic situation or set of circumstances is one that is the opposite of what would be expected. Give proof that Paul is a "pathological liar." (par. 18) Why is this ironic? (HINT! Which of the three boys would have the least reason to lie?)

3. Read each of the following and explain what impression they give of Paul.

   "Paul came out of the Quik Pik sucking on a bottle of pop." (par. 19)

   "Paul loped in long strides to our side of the street." (par. 21)

   "He smiled in a silly way and bobbed his head up and down." (par. 23)

   "He rocked back and forth and started talking." (par. 27)

4. Paul said that his father bought the motorcycle from an ex-Hell's Angels. (par. 32) What does this tell us about Paul?

5. Why do you think that Paul's invitation to Kevin to see the motorcycle is *half-hearted*. (par. 46). Give evidence from the story.

6. After the bike is reported missing, Paul calls the narrator to inform him that the bike has been stolen. The narrator comments, " There wasn't much the police could do. They interviewed the neighbours..." (par. 67). Comment on the use of the word *interviewed*. Do you think the police would have *interviewed* Kevin?

7. Explain the image: "White flesh of broken alder branches showed against the black shadows of leaves." (par. 82). Why do you think the author used these words?

8. What happens to Kevin at the end of the story?

ORAL DISCUSSION

1. Explain the relationships among the three boys and relate it to the plot.
2. The author has created vivid word-pictures of the three main characters. Describe how he wants his readers to feel about each of them.
3. Each of the three boys comes from a different type of family. Explain each boy's home life. Discuss what effect these family backgrounds have on the psychology of each of the boys.
4. Comment on and explain the significance of the contrast of the following physical settings:

> Out behind the McPhadden house were two early seventies model Chev Impalas, big wide boats of cars. The only thing wrong with these cars was that they didn't run. They had seized up from disuse. Each night from mid-May to October, a red and black wool blanket wrapped about him, Kevin made his bed in one or the other of the cars. (par. 9)
>
> They lived in a Red Row house, an old mining company house exactly like mine. At Kevin's place, twenty people shared the same amount of space I often complained was too small for my parents, my kid brother, and me. (par.8)
>
> Valley Woods was the kind of neighbourhood the Brady Bunch lived in. I had seen Valley Woods plenty of times before, but always from the back end: picnic tables, clotheslines, lawn mowers, jungle gyms. (par. 49)

ORAL ACTIVITY

A **eulogy** is a speech written in honour of a person who has died. Prepare and present a eulogy for Kevin written by any one of the following characters: Paul Semple, the narrator, Mrs. Semple, or Mrs. McPhadden

TOOLS OF THE TRADE

Analyzing Setting

In the last chapter, you learned that an essential element in a literary analysis is a discussion of character. Another important element in an analysis is the **setting** in which a story takes place. Writers make a conscious choice about the setting they create. It adds information about the characters and establishes the atmosphere and sociological and/or cultural context of the story.

In order to analyze setting, you must look at the time and place of the story. As with a character analysis, an analysis of setting is not a mere description of the setting but rather a discussion of how the setting is used to provide conditions in which conflicts can arise as well as motivation for the characters' actions.

WRITTEN EXERCISE

Analyze the setting of "Gold Wings " by answering the following questions.

The Starting Point

1. Where did the story take place? (country, city, neighborhood, building, room)
2. When did the story take place? What is the time span?
3. What is the cultural context (social, economic and political) of this story?

The Deeper Analysis

1. How well the setting is developed?
   - is it realistic? – is it complete? – is it accurate?
2. What role does the setting play in the plot?
   - could the action take place in another time and location?
3. In what way does the setting tell you:
   - who the characters are?
   - why they do what they do?

As you read the following poem, consider the importance of the author's choice of setting.

On Saint-Urbain Street

by Milton Acorn

Mr room's bigger than a coffin
but not so well made.
The couple on my left drink, and
at two a.m. the old man shouts
of going back to Russia.
About five he or his wrung-out wife
puke up their passage money.

The janitor (pay, five a week
plus a one-bed apartment

with furnace in kitchen) has
one laughing babe at home
and two girls, for lack of room,
in the orphanage.
On holidays they appear
with their soul-smashed faces.

Upstairs the Negro girl
answers the phone, sings my name
in a voice like a bad angel's.
Her boyfriends change
every weekend, like the movies.
But my room's cheap, tho'
when the wind shifts north
I wear my overcoat
to type this bitter little poem.

VOCABULARY AND COMPREHENSION

1. Why does the author use the word *coffin* in the description of the size of his room?

2. What do the words *wrung-out* tell you about the Russian man's wife?

3. Why does the author refer to the janitor's daughters' faces as *soul-smashed*?

4. Why did the author include the adjective *bitter* in the description of his poem?

ORAL DISCUSSION

1. What words or phrases give a clue about the time in history in which this poem was written?
2. How is it possible to ascertain the living conditions in the apartment building on St. Urbain Street?
3. What do the descriptions of the residents of the apartment building tell you about the socio-economic class of the neighborhood in which the building is located?

WRITING CHALLENGE

Using the **TOOLS OF THE TRADE** discussed above, plan and write an analysis of the setting of either "Gold Wings" or "On St. Urbain Street."

The following question now has significance for you.
Add it to the **Writer's Tool Box** at the beginning of your book.

HAVE I INCLUDED AN ANALYSIS OF SETTING AS PART OF MY SHORT STORY ANALYSIS?

CHAPTER 8

Theme

Just as plot tells what happens in a story, character tells who is in the story, and setting tells where the story takes place, **theme** *tells why the story was written.*

Short stories may either present an idea, raise an issue or convey a message. These ideas, issues or messages may be evident enough to allow for a consensus among all readers or deliberately vague in order to allow readers to interpret them according to their own life experiences. Whether the theme is directly stated or not, literary analysis demands that any interpretation of theme be supported through reference to plot, characters and or setting.

For example in the short story "Monkey On My Back," among the numerous themes are the following:

All families have their idiosyncrasies.

This statement of theme can be supported by referring to conflicts in the plot (Aunt Mabel's incarceration, the Chinese restaurant, cousin Barbara and her transvestite monkey), the characters and their various eccentricities (Fred's television mania, and Aunt Ruth's drinking), and the setting (Aunt Anna's run-down farm and Crinklewood's loss of the Maraschino Cherry factory.)

You should form your own judgments about people.

This statement can be supported by referring to the reason for the narrator's visit to Crinklewood in the first place, and his subsequent realization about the veracity of his mother's comments.

PRE-READING

1. Do you have any childhood memories about a time when your family moved to a new location?
2. How are new immigrants often treated in their new country?
3. When you have traveled, have you ever had trouble adjusting to the culture?

The following short story is set in a small Albertan town.

Bugs

by Nancy Holmes

1 It was raining the night I discovered the bugs.

2 In the dark, the old house smelled wet and musty. My little sister, a warm, sleeping solid, kept rolling into me as I lay rigid in bed listening to the rain hiss on the roof, the dank odour of our new home filling my nostrils.

3 I was squeezing my eyes shut, trying to blank out all memory of my first day at school in the new town. But instead of fading the ugly whisper grew louder until it rang like a shout in my head. "Dirty Bohunk" someone had said softly in my ear as I crouched over a bench in the crowded cloakroom pulling on my rainboots.

4 I was too restless to sleep. Around midnight I got out of bed and crept down the hall. The cold floor cracked loudly beneath my bare feet and I hurried to the bathroom, closing the door behind me before I searched for the light switch. I didn't want to wake Mom or Daddy: they would see my raw eyes and would ask what was wrong. I was too ashamed to tell them about the whisper in the cloakroom. As if they wouldn't have understood.

5 We'd only been living in the house for two days and I had trouble finding the bathroom switch in the dark. The damp smell of the walls was thick and stifling as if someone were holding a dirty wash rag over my face. I found the light and I flicked it on.

6 Then I saw them. Thousands of crawling black bugs. A thin sprinkling of insects shifting all over the walls and ceiling. As soon as the light hit them, they sifted into the wall, swiftly poured into dark corners, behind the toilet and into the wooden trim around the door and window.

7 I screamed and by the time my parents arrived, the bugs had completely disappeared.

8 Daddy, tall and spindly in his long underwear, looked at me in disbelief when I described the bugs. I was aware of his bony limbs, a large expanse of hairy chest, his naked feet, white and gnarled, and was suddenly embarrassed to be in the small bathroom with him in his underwear and me in my nightdress. I clung to Mom while he inspected the walls and the corners, shadows making his thin nose and cheekbones sharp and elongated like some villain in the silent movies.

9 I buried my face in Mom's faded pink nightgown. Her large hands were warm as they held me and stroked my hair. She clucked and cooed, her voice husky with her accent, her breast full of scent: a mixture of yeast, cabbage and rose perfume.

10 Daddy sent me back to bed.

11 "I'll keep a lookout for these bugs of yours." He glanced at Mom, shaking his head slightly.

12 I slipped back under the covers and fell asleep immediately, as if I had absorbed sleepiness from my mother's soft skin.

13 Mom and Daddy thought I was having a nightmare and the bugs were a bad dream. Unfortunately as the days went by, the house revealed its infestation to everyone.

14 It was a cold, wet autumn and the house swelled up like a bloated body. For the insects, the humidity created perfect breeding conditions. The rotten eaves, sweating walls, sagging floors were riddled with bugs and soon everyone in the family had come across them in some chilly corner. The insects were extremely light shy, never oozing out of the walls unless the room was dark. And each night there seemed to be more of them.

15 Mom wanted to move.

16 "All my things! All my things!" she cried, gathering her cheap, colourful icons into her arms and sealing them away in chests jammed with mothballs; rushing from room to room, her long skirts sweeping, as she moved all her furniture several feel away from the walls as if the bugs were less likely to get at it there.

17 Daddy patted her arm and ignored her weeping.

18 "Anna, calm down. I will make the landlady fumigate the place."

19 Daddy wasn't Ukrainian at all: he was Polish. There is a difference, I've always thought, like the difference between the Irish and the English. The Ukrainians have a streak of Cossack violence. Every emotion is lavish and charged. My mother was sentimental, warm, open. She loved colour, sad songs, lots of good food, and boisterous weddings and funerals. Daddy was reserved and sober. He and all his relatives wore dark clothes and lots of them, as if always bundled up for a bleak Eastern European winter.

20 However, back then, in the early 1920's, "Bohunks" were Poles and Ukrainians alike. Our family was definitely "Bohunk" and our landlady wouldn't fumigate our house.

21 Daddy came home from work one night in a rage. His blue eyes were narrow and bitter.

22 "The bitch," I was shocked to hear him say. "The stupid bitch. Implies all the time I talk to her that *we're* dirty! That *we've* brought the bugs with us! This house is so infested it must have taken years for it to get this bad! Yet she has the . I'll prove it to her. I'll drag her here to see those bugs if I have to . . . to knock her out first!"

23 The ugly whisper of the cloakroom crawled into my head again. "Dirty Bohunk." I left the room where Mom and Daddy were talking loudly and angrily, not wanting to hear anymore about the landlady.

24 Her name was Mrs. Murray and she came to inspect the house one morning when Daddy was at work and I was home sick although I think the cold was largely invention. I began to dream up excuses to stay home, thinking the kids at school, those with English names, were staring at me and whispering behind my back.

25 Mrs. Murray hadn't bothered to dress up to make her visit. I saw her curling rags under her scarf and she wore a dingy, flannel housecoat under her rain gear. She had lovely round

blue eyes with long black lashes but her face, perhaps once as attractive as her eyes, had deteriorated. Her skin was broken by faint blue and red veins; her lips were puffed with bruises. Years later I heard that her husband beat her and that she drank but I hated her with a simple purity the morning she walked into our kitchen, not even scraping the mud off her boots, her mouth pursed and smug as she informed my mother that she was the landlady.

26 "Well where are these bugs of yours?" Her voice slurred slightly.

27 Mom pulled up a chair for her, trying to explain the bugs only came out at night. Her accent became thicker with anxiety. Mrs. Murray pretended not to understand what she was saying.

28 Ignoring the offer of the chair, the landlady tramped into the living room in her muddy boots, took one quick look at the walls then returned to the kitchen, speaking to my mother in a loud, slow voice.

29 "No bugs here. You tell your husband that. Understand? No bugs here." Then she spoke more normally, noticing me huddled in a chair by the stove. "At least there weren't any before you moved in. You just keep the place clean, dear. Sweep the floors, wash the walls. You're living in town now, not on the farm."

30 Mom nodded Mrs. Murray out the door, twisting her hands and mumbling. As soon as the woman left, Mom burst into noisy tears and spent the rest of the morning scrubbing the floor which the landlady had streaked with mud. I went to my bed to read a library book, blushing every time I thought of Mrs. Murray — angry at her for saying my mother was dirty: Mom who even scrubbed the front door and who swept out the yard, Mom whose hands were perpetually red from washing and rinsing. I was angry with Mom too, for nodding so eagerly, for being so fearful. I ignored her when she came up to my room to offer comfort, company and hot tea.

31 Even then Daddy wouldn't move. He would make Mrs. Murray apologize, admit her mistake. He vowed to prove the existence of the bugs.

32 For a week he tore up floorboards, peeled off baseboards, drilled holes in the plaster and unscrewed light sockets, looking for evidence of the bugs: nests, eggs, droppings, dead shells, anything. Mom swept up after him, pleading, scolding, but he brushed her complaints aside even when he found no substantial proof.

33 Next he borrowed a camera and flash from one of his cousins, a pharmacist in Vegreville. It was a small, black box with an accordian-type front. We sat up til ten o'clock that night. It was like a holiday. Daddy was excited and nervous, shooing us away from the camera balanced on a tippy tripod; he fiddled with the viewfinder, adjusted the flash. Mom made us kids hot milk and cookies and kept saying "Hush" when we giggled or squealed in the dark, as if the bugs, who came out every night regardless of the noise level, would be scared away by rowdy children. I think she enjoyed herself that night; victory seemed imminent. She cheered and clapped when the flash went off and Daddy cleared his brow with a handkerchief, smiling proudly as we clamoured around begging him to take a picture of the family now that the business was over. I still have that photo — slightly overexposed, grey and grizzled like the weather that autumn. Mom looks unusually stern and we children are shyly dishevelled. I, the eldest, am tall and adolescently weedy, wearing a wilting aster in my hair which at the time I thought looked chic. The next day I wore one to school but after enduring the giggles of my classmates all morning I tore it out of my hair and threw it in the garbage.

34 That weekend Daddy and his cousin developed the pictures. They were failures. The white walls had reflected so much of the flash that the bugs were flooded out. Daddy wouldn't try it again — I suspect his pride was hurt that his photos turned out so bad.

35 By now Daddy was obsessed with the bugs. "Evidence" he went around the house muttering. "Proof." He refused to hire an exterminator with our own money though Mom suggested this frequently.

36 "It's the principle, Anna. The principle," he told her and I, thinking of "Dirty Bohunk," agreed with him.

37 Mom began to hate the house. On the farm she had coddled and loved her home. The kitchen had been filled with the warm, sweet weight of food smells — bread, cabbage rolls, doughnuts, poppyseed cake, sizzling bacon, fruity stuffs being preserved. Now she spent every day cleaning, cleaning, cleaning. She changed the sheets on our bed each morning, washed the walls, beat the rugs. I remember thinking resentfully that we always had potatoes and sausages for supper. And I remember Mom always looked tired.

38 There were arguments every night with Mom shouting, crying, pleading and Daddy murmuring or saying loudly, "That's enough, Anna."

39 One drizzly night I woke up from a fitful sleep. That day in the schoolyard the clannish group of English girls were pointing at me and my new skirt, several inches too long. Mom always made my dresses long, in spite of my protests. When she was a girl it had been a mark of growing up to be able to wear longer skirts. She couldn't understand that styles had changed. Even in my sleep I seemed to hear a constant whispered titter that made me squirm.

40 I heard Mom moving around in the kitchen, in the dark. I thought I heard matches being struck.

41 Daddy called out from the bedroom down the hall, "Anna, come to bed. It's after one in the morning."

42 "Go to sleep. I'm busy," Mom answered.

43 I wondered if she were stalking the bugs, her old enemies. Perhaps praying about them or damning them with some old Ukrainian curse. After listening to Mom shuffle around in the kitchen for several minutes, the rain drumming on the roof put me to sleep again.

44 The morning broke clear, clean and wet like cold water. I could hear sparrows chitter and clipping drops of water dripped from the eaves and the trees. The sunshine was bright and windy, flapping like a thousand bright flags. The rain had stopped.

45 The house looked almost cheerful I thought, with the sun making the water-stained walls nearly white.

46 I met Daddy in the hallway as we came out of our rooms together. He nodded and smiled stiffly.

47 "Morning."

48 I remember thinking the sunny weather was making Daddy uncommonly cheerful as he rarely did more than grunt in the morning. I remember feeling very grown-up because I was amused by my father.

49 I stepped into the kitchen, still smiling, and saw my mother asleep at the table. The sunlight pouring through the icy clean windows made the kerchief on her head glow red and warm like blood. Her large, white arms were wrapped around her face as she rested her head on the table. A small, empty cardboard box lay beside her.

50 I wondered why she was asleep in the kitchen instead of in her bed.

51 Then I saw the wall behind her. It dazzled white in the early morning sun. I began screaming.

52 Mom stirred and woke.

53 "Be quiet," she jumped up from the table and began shaking me. I gulped back my screams, shocked by her rough grip.

54 "Be quiet both of you," she shouted as my father started to say something, angrily. She turned on him, letting go of my arm abruptly, as if she had forgotten all about me, pointing at the wall behind her. "That's your proof. Your proof. You understand? Now get that woman and show her your precious bugs and get her to clean my house! Get my house cleaned!"

55 Mom's face was fierce and hot. I looked away and stared again at the wall.

56 It was covered with dead bugs. Each brittle black body was stuck to the wall with a thin pin. Hundreds of dead black bugs pinned to the wall.

57 I turned to my father, wanting him to say something sane, angry, wanting him to put his arm around me, to get me away from Mom who suddenly seemed violent and unreliable.

58 Instead his hands dropped at his sides and his eyes looked washed with age.

59 "I'm sorry, Anna. It's their stupidity. Makes me stupid . . ." he whispered hoarsely.

60 She opened her arms and he went to her. Holding him tightly, she looked over his sunken shoulder at me, her eyes stern and passionate, motioning for me to leave them alone.

61 I slowly walked out of the kitchen, leaving my father to his comfort. We moved a few days later.

VOCABULARY AND COMPREHENSION

1. Determine the meaning of the word *cloakroom* in paragraph 3.

2. "As soon as the light hit them, they *sifted* into the wall, swiftly *poured* into dark corners..." (par. 6) What do the italicized verbs mean?

3. "The rotten eaves, sweating walls, sagging floors were riddled with bugs and soon everyone in the family had come across them in some chilly corner." (par. 14)

   What does this description of the narrator's home tell you about the economic situation of the family?

4. Vegreville is a small town in Alberta, Canada.

   Where does the narrator's mother come from originally? ______________________

   The narrator's father? ______________________

5. Mrs. Murray, the landlord, comes visit the family. " 'Well where are these bugs of yours?' Her voice *slurred* slightly."(par. 26) What does the word *slurred* tell you about Mrs. Murray?

   ____

6. "Mom nodded Mrs. Murray out the door, twisting her hands and mumbling." (par. 30) What does this scene tell you about the mother?

   In your opinion, why didn't the mother react with anger?

   ____

   ____

7. "Daddy was excited and nervous, *shooing us away* from the camera balanced on a *tippy tripod...*" (par. 33)

   What does *shooing us away* mean? ______________________

   What is a *tippy tripod*? ______________________

8. How is the following image effective in describing the mother's state of mind when the daughter finds her in the kitchen. "The sunlight pouring through the icy clean windows made the kerchief on her head glow red and warm like blood. Her large, white arms were wrapped around her face as she rested her head on the table." (par. 49) Comment on the power of this image?

   ____

   ____

9. "I gulped back my screams, shocked by her rough grip." (par. 53) Why was the narrator afraid of her mother in this scene?

   ____

ORAL DISCUSSION

1. The story opens with a description of the place, the main characters, and the main problem.
   Where does the action occur? Who are the main characters? What is the main problem?

2. As the story progresses, the narrator frequently refers to the term 'dirty Bohunk'. How is the narrator different from the other children? How does she feel about the word *Bohunk*?
3. What is the type of conflict that occurs in this story? What evidence is there from the story to support this?
4. Look closely at paragraphs 25 to 29. What does Mrs. Murray think of the narrator's family?
5. Why does the father insist on proving the existence of the bugs to Mrs. Murray, when his wife simply wants to move away?
6. As the father presses on to prove to the landlord the existence of the bugs, why does the narrator support his actions?
7. What is the climax in this story?
8. How does the narrator react to the mother's bug-pinning? How does the father react?
9. What do you think the author's theme or message is?

TOOLS OF THE TRADE

Analyzing Theme

When searching for the theme in a piece of writing, you must ask yourself the following questions:

* *What do I think the author's intent was?*
* *What issues does the author deal with?*

In an analysis of theme, you should consider a number of factors:

* *Theme must be expressed in the form of a statement.* "Escape" could be considered the subject of the story "Gold Wings," but it is not a statement of theme. The statement of theme could be "Regardless of an environment or economic situation, everyone needs to escape sometimes." Avoid reducing your statement of theme to a **cliché**, such as "Life is like a bowl of cherries; it's the pits."
* *Theme expresses a generalization about life.* The major details in the story must relate in some way to your statement of theme.
* *Some stories may have more than one theme.* When doing an analysis of theme, it is important that you can support your statement with evidence from the text.

In an analysis of theme you can determine the following:

* *the type of theme* (sociological, or cultural, psychological, political, or a combination).
* *how the theme is developed* What role do the plot, characters and setting play in the theme's development? If you cannot find enough evidence to support the theme, it is possible that either you have not found the theme of the story or perhaps the author has not successfully developed the theme.

WRITING CHALLENGE

1. Using the **TOOLS OF THE TRADE** presented above, write an analysis of a theme for the short story "Bugs." Remember that you must support your analysis with quotations from the story.
2. Write a text in which you respond to one of the following statements:
   * Everyone has felt like a "bohunk" at one point in their lives.
   * It is impossible to live in a prejudice-free society.

The following question now has significance for you.
Add it to the **Writer's Tool Box** at the beginning of your book.

HAVE I INCLUDED AN ANALYSIS OF THEME AS PART OF MY SHORT STORY ANALYSIS?

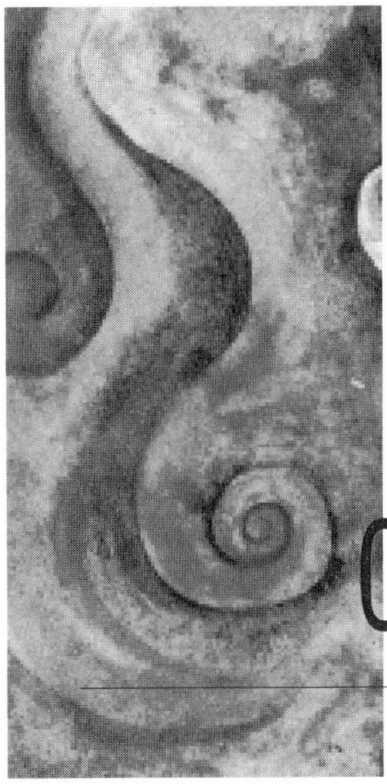

CHAPTER 9

Comparison and Contrast

The technique of **comparison** and **contrast** is used to show the *similarities* and *differences* between two or more different works. (The two works *must have something significant in common* that can be compared, yet they *must also have differences that can be contrasted.*) The elements chosen to be compared and contrasted will depend on the works in question. For example, you may choose to compare and contrast elements of two works from similar genres (novel to novel, short story to short story). You might also compare and contrast two different genres such as a movie and the novel that inspired it. When you do this, you compare and contrast:

PLOT

CHARACTER

SETTING

THEME

TOOLS OF THE TRADE

The Thesis Statement and Comparison and Contrast

The first step in creating a comparison and contrast is to establish your thesis or main goal. Once you have decided on why you are doing the comparison and contrast, you must then determine what aspects of each work can be used to best support your thesis.

In your thesis statement you may choose to compare and contrast two works with similar themes, but different characters, settings and plots. For example, two pieces that deal with the theme of prejudice may have wildly different plots, characters and settings, but the point of your comparison and contrast would be *to highlight how each author explored the same theme*. The superiority of one version over another is not necessarily stated.

Alternatively, you may make a value judgement. For example, if you are comparing the novel *Forrest Gump* with the movie, you should begin by stating that one version is superior to the other in some way. In the development of your thesis you could demonstrate through a comparison and contrast of plot, character, setting and theme how one piece is superior to the other.

As with all writing, it is important to invest time in planning a comparison and contrast essay. Below you will find an organizational outline that can help you to plan your essay.

INTRODUCTION

Name the two works in question and develop your introduction using the strategies discussed in Chapter 3. Remember to state your thesis clearly.

Title 1 (First Work) ____________________

Title 2 (Second Work) ____________________

<Thesis Statement>

____

____

Body 1

<ASPECT 1>

____________ ____________ ____________

____________ How do they differ or ____________

____________ how are they the same? ____________

Body 2

<ASPECT 2>

__________ __________ __________

__________ How do they differ or __________

__________ how are they the same? __________

Body 3

<ASPECT 3>

__________ __________ __________

__________ How do they differ or __________

__________ how are they the same? __________

(Aspects one, two and three must all support your thesis statement.)

CONCLUSION

Make a conclusion based on the comparison and contrast using the strategies discussed in Chapter 4.

____

____

____

Within each paragraph (body 1, body 2, body 3), you must compare and contrast various aspects that support your thesis statement. Each paragraph must have a clear topic sentence (see Chapter 2) that tells the reader what element will be treated in that paragraph. Also you should make sure that each paragraph is clear and cohesive and that it flows smoothly. This can be done by using transitional words and phrases.

TRANSITIONAL WORDS AND PHRASES USED FOR COMPARISON

To Show Differences	*To Show Similarities*
in contrast	also
but	likewise
contrary to	similarly
however	the same is true
on the other hand	in a similar way

RAPUNZEL

1 Once upon a time there was a husband and wife who for quite some time had been wishing in vain for a child. Finally, the dear Lord gave the wife a sign of hope that their wish would be fulfilled. Now in the back of their house the couple had a small window that overlooked a splendid garden filled with the most beautiful flowers and herbs. The garden, however, was surrounded by a high wall, and nobody dared enter it because it belonged to a sorceress who was very powerful and feared by all. One day when the wife was standing at the window and looking down into the garden, she noticed a bed of the finest rapunzel lettuce. The lettuce looked so fresh and green that her mouth watered, and she had a great craving to eat some. Day by day this craving increased, and since she knew she could not get any, she began to waste away and look pale and miserable.

2 Her husband became alarmed and asked, "What's wrong with you, dear wife?"

3 "Ah," she responded, "I shall certainly die if I don't get any of that rapunzel from the garden behind our house."

4 Her husband, who loved her, thought, Before I let my wife die, I'll do anything I must to make sure she gets some rapunzel.

5 That day at dusk he climbed over the wall into the garden of the sorceress, hastily grabbed a handful of rapunzel, and brought them to his wife. Immediately she made them into a salad and ate it with great zest. But the rapunzel tasted so good to her, so very good, that her desire for them was three times greater by the next day. If she was to have any peace, her husband knew he had to climb into the garden once more. So at dusk he scaled the wall again, and just as he landed on the other side, he was given a tremendous scare, for he stood face-to-face with the sorceress.

6 "How dare you climb into my garden and steal my rapunzel like a thief?" she said with an angry look. "You'll pay for this!"

7 "Oh," he cried, "Please, let mercy prevail over justice. I did this only because I was in a predicament: my wife noticed your rapunzel from our window, and she developed such a great craving for it that she would have died if I hadn't brought her some to eat."

8 Upon hearing that, the anger of the sorceress subsided, and she said to him, "If it's truly as you say, then I shall permit you to take as many rapunzel as you like, but only under one condition: when your wife gives birth, I must have the child. You needn't fear about the child's well-being, for I shall take care of it like a mother."

9 In his fear the man agreed to everything, and when his wife had the baby, the sorceress appeared at once. She gave the child the name Rapunzel and took her away.

10 Rapunzel grew to be the most beautiful child under the sun. But when she was twelve years old, the sorceress locked her in a tower that was in a forest. It had neither door nor stairs, only a little window high above. Whenever the sorceress wanted to get in, she would stand below and call out:

11 "Rapunzel, Rapunzel,
Let down your hair for me."

12 Rapunzel's hair was long and radiant, as fine as spun gold. Every time she heard the voice of the sorceress, she unpinned her braids and wound them around a hook on the window. Then she let her hair drop twenty yards, and the sorceress would climb up on it.

13 A few years later a king's son happened to be riding through the forest and passed by the tower. Suddenly, he heard a song so lovely that he stopped to listen. It was Rapunzel, who passed the time in her solitude by letting her sweet voice resound in the forest. The prince wanted to climb up to her, and he looked for a door but could not find one. So he rode home. However, the song had touched his heart so deeply that he rode out into the forest every day and listened. One time, as he was standing behind a tree, he saw the sorceress approach and heard her call out:

14 "Rapunzel, Rapunzel,
Let down your hair for me."

15 Then Rapunzel let down her braids, and the sorceress climbed up to her.

16 "If that's the ladder one needs to get up there, I'm also going to try my luck," the prince declared.

17 The next day, as it began to get dark, he went to the tower and called out:

18 "Rapunzel, Rapunzel,
Let down your hair for me."

19 All at once the hair dropped down, and the prince climbed up. When he entered the tower, Rapunzel was at first terribly afraid, for she had never laid eyes on a man before. However, the prince began to talk to her in a friendly way and told her that her song had touched his heart so deeply that he had not been able to rest until he had seen her. Rapunzel

then lost her fear, and when he asked her whether she would have him for her husband, and she saw that he was young and handsome, she thought, He'll certainly love me better than old Mother Gothel. So she said yes and placed her hand in his.

20 "I want to go with you very much," she said, "but I don't know how I can get down. Every time you come, you must bring a skein of silk with you, and I'll weave it into a ladder. When it's finished, then I'll climb down, and you can take me away on your horse."

21 They agreed that until then he would come to her every evening, for the old woman came during the day. Meanwhile, the sorceress did not notice anything, until one day Rapunzel blurted out, "Mother Gothel, how is it that you're much heavier than the prince? When I pull him up, he's here in a second."

22 "Ah, you godless child!" exclaimed the sorceress. "What's this I hear? I thought I had made sure you had no contact with the outside world, but you've deceived me!"

23 In her fury she seized Rapunzel's beautiful hair, wrapped it around her left hand several times, grabbed a pair of scissors with her right hand, and *snip, snap* the hair was cut off, and the beautiful braids lay on the ground. Then the cruel sorceress took Rapunzel to a desolate land where she had to live in great misery and grief.

24 On the same day that she had banished Rapunzel, the sorceress fastened the braids that she had cut off to the hook on the window, and that evening, when the prince came and called out:

25 "Rapunzel, Rapunzel,
Let down your hair for me."

26 she let the hair down.

27 The prince climbed up, but instead of finding his dearest Rapunzel on top, he found the sorceress, who gave him vicious and angry looks.

28 "Aha!" she exclaimed with contempt. "You want to fetch your darling wife, but the beautiful bird is no longer sitting in the nest, and she won't be singing anymore. The cat has got her, and it will also scratch out your eyes. Rapunzel is lost to you, and you will never see her again!"

29 The prince was beside himself with grief, and in his despair he jumped off the tower. He escaped with his life, but the thorns he fell into pierced his eyes, so he became blind. Now he strayed about in the forest, ate nothing but roots and berries, and did nothing but mourn and weep about the loss of his dearest wife. Thus he wandered for many years in misery. Eventually, he made his way to the desolate land where Rapunzel was leading a wretched existence with the twins, a boy and a girl, to whom she had given birth. When he heard a voice that he thought sounded familiar, he went straight toward it, and when he reached her, Rapunzel recognized him. She embraced him and wept, and as two of her tears dropped on his eyes they became clear, and he could see again. Then he escorted her back to his kingdom, where he was received with joy, and they lived happily and contentedly for a long time thereafter.

Bad Girl

by David Arnason

1 Once upon a time in a small town just near the Saskatchewan border, there lived a very disobedient girl. Her name was Ellen, and she was in grade twelve. She wanted to go to university to study music and become a famous singer, but her mother wanted her to get a job in town as a clerk in the Co-op store, and her father wanted her to stay on the farm and help her mother with the milking and the chickens. They were both deeply religious people, and they were afraid that if Ellen went out into the wide world, she would lose her religion and come to harm.

2 "I don't know how many times I've told you," her mother would say, "but I'm telling you again. If you wear your skirts as short as you do, you are asking for trouble."

3 "Don't talk back to me, young woman," her father said almost every day. "And don't flash your eyes at me. I know insolence when I see it, and I won't tolerate it, do you understand?"

4 Ellen knew she was disobedient. She was supposed to pray in a soft voice at the beginning of each class, but she hadn't done so for years, and nothing had happened to her. She had sneaked off and gone to a movie with the other kids, and God had not struck her dead. She'd even had a glass of whisky with some of the boys at a dance to which she had been forbidden to go, and she had not got drunk and the police had not caught her.

5 In fact, it seemed that the only bad things that ever happened to her were delivered by her own parents. Ellen's mother liked to slap her when she didn't work hard enough. Her father beat her whenever he found out that she'd done something he didn't like. But everybody else in town was good to her, and they all loved to hear her sing. They said things like, "You've got the voice of an angel. You should study and become an opera singer."

6 Her parents warned her that God watched her every move, and that he would not be mocked. He would deliver pain for disobedience.

7 "If that's the case," Ellen said to herself, "then my parents must be working off a lifetime of disobedience."

8 And that seemed as if it might be true. Her father went to church every Sunday, but the bank was threatening to take away the farm, and he'd broken his leg when he rolled the tractor, and now he walked with a painful limp. Her mother had varicose veins and some sort of stomach disease that made her breath smell so bad that nobody wanted to sit next to her, not even in church. If they were God's chosen, Ellen decided, then she'd just as soon escape his notice.

9 Ellen got straight A's in grade twelve. School work came easy to her, and she liked the classroom, where everyone was polite to each other, and where you really did seem to get what you deserved. If you worked hard, you got an A. If you didn't, you got a B or a C, if you didn't do anything at all, you failed.

10 Ellen's biggest disobedience was the secret bank account she kept. She was working part-time at the Co-op and saving up to go to university. If she won a couple of scholarships, she was sure that she could do it. Her greatest fear was that her parents might find out about her bank account and seize it. It would be a month until she turned eighteen, and she wasn't sure whether her parents could steal her money or not. The one thing she was certain about

was that if they found out, religious or not, they would take her money from her.

11 The other problem was Larry. Larry was madly in love with Ellen and he wanted to marry her. Ellen knew that her parents would forbid the marriage at first, but she was pretty certain that they'd finally give in. It was the one place that she was hoping for their rigidity. If she married Larry, then she would never be a famous singer. She would be a farm wife just like her mother, and she would become dry and mean and get varicose veins and bad breath.

12 About a month earlier, Larry had become so insistent about marrying her that the only way she could convince him not to go to her father and ask for her hand was to sleep with him. Or not so much sleep with as have sex with in the back seat of his Chevy. Ellen had been worried that she would get pregnant, and her mother had warned her so often about sex that she assumed it would be a painful and horrible experience.

13 It turned out to be the most fun she'd ever had. She couldn't believe how nice it was, and after the first time, she walked around like Marco Polo must have when he discovered China. She could hardly think about anything else, and for a couple of weeks, she didn't do anything to anger either of her parents. She almost agreed to marry Larry.

14 Her father noticed her change of mood and became very watchful. He drove his pickup into town and spied on Ellen when she went for lunch to the Chinese café, and he insisted that she come right home from school and not go out in the evening. Ellen didn't care. She had sex with Larry standing up in the janitor's room during study period.

15 Ellen's father talked to Ellen's mother, and Ellen's mother took her aside and talked to her about sex. Ellen could barely stand the smell of her mother's breath, but she listened.

16 "I just want you to be careful," her mother said. "If you lose your reputation, then nobody will want to marry you. Your father and I would just die if you got pregnant. We couldn't hold up our heads in church. And don't think it's any great deal. It's something a woman has to suffer, and there's no point to starting suffering any sooner than you need. And you are the church organist. Remember that."

17 Ellen did not forget that she was the church organist. It was the single good thing that she could say about the church. Her father would never have let her continue to take lessons if it weren't that it made him look good at church. Sometimes, when she was playing a hymn and she saw her father standing in the first pew, singing off-key in his whiny voice, she imagined him keeling over with a heart attack. She wouldn't even stop playing. She'd switch into something joyful and triumphant with great crescendos.

18 Ellen felt that the best way to avoid suspicion was to be as disobedient as her parents wanted. So she didn't do the dishes she was supposed to do, and she didn't feed the calves, and her mother slapped her. She took the car without permission on a Sunday afternoon and made love to Larry in a haystack, and got back late for supper. Her father beat her with his belt, and made her pray on her knees for two hours, but he stopped following her around and spying on her with his binoculars.

19 When the school year came to an end, the principal told her father that she'd won a thousand-dollar scholarship.

20 "Good," her father said. "She can buy herself a couple of calves and raise them over the winter." The principal told him that she could only use the money to go to the university.

21 "How about Bible College?" her father asked.

22 "Well, yes, I suppose," the principal answered. "But I thought she wanted to study music."

23 "Got her heart set on Bible college," her father said, and he went home and announced to Ellen that she would be attending Thorncrest Pentecostal Bible College.

24 "Got your heart set on an education. Well, this is the only education that really counts," he told her. "It'll teach you a little about authority and discipline."

25 Ellen felt that she would sooner go to prison than to Bible college. She would sooner work in the Co-op or help around the farm. But it gave her an excuse to apply to the university. You had to be accepted at the university to get into Thorncrest, she would tell her parents if they asked. She had applied for several bursaries and a government loan, and when the letters of reply came from the university, she managed to sneak the answers by her father by getting to the mailbox first and hiding the responses in her room.

26 In the meanwhile, Larry was nearly frantic about her going away to the city to study at Bible college. He wanted her to stay home and marry him, and when she told him that she wasn't ready to make that sort of commitment and maybe they could just be friends, he wept and then raged, and told her that she'd be married to him by fall, just you wait and see.

27 Things came to a crisis the day before her birthday. Larry caught her on the way back from the Co-op, and announced that he couldn't live without her, and that if she didn't agree to marry him, he was going to kill her and commit suicide. He showed her the shotgun he had bought for the occasion. Ellen agreed to marry him of course, but she convinced him not to tell her parents until the morning of her birthday. He agreed to wait a day, but no longer.

28 When she got home, her father was waiting for her. He waved a sheaf of papers at her. "I've been in your room," he said. "Checking for drugs because you've been acting so strange. And I found these."

29 "Those are my applications for Thorncrest College."

30 "It doesn't say Thorncrest College. It says university."

31 Ellen wasn't sure how much her father knew about the application process, but her only hope was to bluff. "It has to say university. First you get accepted to the university. Then when you get there, you fill out a form for Thorncrest College."

32 "Well it don't explain this," he said, waving her bankbook in the air. "It don't explain how you got four thousand dollars in the bank."

33 "I earned it, working at the Co-op and babysitting. It's my money." Ellen's heart sank as she saw her hopes for escape dimming. Even Larry suddenly loomed as hope.

34 "Stole it you mean," her father said. "You've been eating my food and living in my house with all that money in the bank and me nearly crazy trying to find a way to feed you. You owe me that for room and board."

35 "Your father's right," her mother chimed in. "That's properly our money."

36 "And we're going straight down to the bank to get it," her father added, and he caught Ellen by the wrist and dragged her out to the pickup. When they got to town, he hauled her from the truck and dragged her to the door.

37 "Now you get that money and bring it directly out," her father said.

38 Ellen reached out her hand and pulled the door handle. It wouldn't open. The tellers in the bank were all at their stations, counting their change, but she could see that the clock on the wall read one minute after three.

39 "It's locked," she said. "It closes at three on Mondays. We'll have to wait until tomorrow."

40 "We're getting it now," her father shouted, and he began to hammer on the door of the bank. At first there was no answer. Finally, the manager came to the door and spoke to them through an electronic box.

41 "We're closed," he said in a tinny electronic voice.

42 "Well, open. We got some banking to do."

43 "I'm sorry. You'll have to wait until tomorrow."

44 "Open that door. We're coming in now." Ellen's father was livid with rage. The manager, on the other side of the glass door, seemed equally livid.

45 "I'm calling the police," he said. "The teller has already called them. You can't force a bank to open when it's closed."

46 "Call them, then," Ellen's father shouted at the door. "They can take away this thieving slut until I get my money back from her." And he turned to glare at the spot where Ellen had been standing only a moment before. There was nobody there, and the pickup was gone.

47 Ellen drove home as fast as she could, skidding on the gravel of the driveway as she rounded the corner. Her mother was out in the barn, or perhaps in the chicken house. At least she wasn't in the house, and Ellen was grateful for that. She tossed clothes at random into a suitcase, and collected all her papers with their acceptances and bursaries and put them in too. Then she put on her shortest skirt and walked to the highway and stuck out her thumb. The first car that came along picked her up and gave her a ride all the way to the city. She stopped at the first bank she came to and used her bank card to withdraw three hundred dollars. Then she spent her first night away from home in a Holiday Inn. She swam in the pool, and she ordered breakfast in bed for the next morning. She felt no guilt. She felt only a sense of peace that she had always known was waiting for her somewhere.

48 Her father disowned her, as she had hoped he would. He put a message in the local paper saying that he was no longer responsible for her debts, and she read it in the university library. But he didn't pursue her any farther, and no police came to her door. Larry disappeared into the past as if he had been erased from a sheet of paper. After the second day, she could hardly remember his face. Ellen moved in with a medical student who thought he was poor, but he paid the rent and he was a decent lover.

49 Ellen did not see Larry or either of her parents after that final day, and she didn't think she ever would. There was, however, one brief electronic moment when they were together. Ellen's parents had gone to the Legion to play bingo. Larry was the caller. At intermission, he turned on the big television at the front of the hall. Ellen appeared on the screen in the role of Carmen. She was dressed in a revealing cotton dress and was sitting on a low stool. Her rich voice filled the hall for just one second before Larry turned the switch and put on the hockey game.

50 Ellen perched carefully on the side of the bed so as not to awaken her lover. From the window of the villa, she could see the sun glint on the Mediterranean waves. Ellen's parents straightened their cards. Larry's voice began, "Under the B, six."

ORAL DISCUSSION

1. What are the similarities and differences between the protagonists in the two stories?
2. Compare and contrast the antagonists in the two stories.
3. How is the boyfriend in "Bad Girl" different from the prince in "Rapunzel." What does this tell you about modern beliefs?
4. The evil witch puts Rapunzel in a tower to cut her off from the rest of the world. What is the Bad Girl's *tower*?
5. What are the secrets in the two stories?
6. What do the two different endings tell you about the social reality in which the stories take place?
7. Do the two stories share a common theme?

WRITING CHALLENGE

In a comparison and contrast essay, respond to the following statement:

While the short story "Bad Girl" is a modern version of the fable "Rapunzel," the differences between the two stories reflect the different times in which they were written.

In your response, compare and contrast the plot, characters, setting and theme of the two stories.

THE BIRTH OF MAX MUELLER — SEPTEMBER 25, 1971

by Cookie Mueller

The night Max was born mongrels roamed in packs. The moon had turned to blood and the hungry hounds were howling for it in wild lunar lust.

I was in pain in the maternity ward of the Hyannis Hospital, but this wasn't plain pain, no; this was the kind of pain that for reasons of sanity, the mind doesn't allow a woman to remember. It was relentless, unbearable, hideous, appalling, horrifying. I was undergoing internal gut ripping tubal wringing, organ stretching, muscle pummeling, bone cracking. I was the grand martyr. Prometheus knew no pain like this. Lamaze had lied.

I couldn't believe that women went through this to have children. After this why would anyone want to have another one?

In my hallucinations caused by pain delirium, I watched dozens of night birds throw themselves, screaming, against the glass of the windows … or was it just hail?

Every sound was magnified. Everything roared.

The fluorescent light was buzzing like a chainsaw, the clock ticking on the wall was Chinese water torture, the cries from other women in the next rooms were as ear-splitting as the wrong songs of distressed Humpback whales. The white tiles on the floor were so clean they were whistling. Even the usually silent plants on the window sill, benevolently doing their miraculous carbon monoxide to oxygen exchange, were wheezing with asthmatic photosynthesis.

From my antiseptic bed with the stiff flash-pasteurized sheets in a severely blank hospital room I could see, through the window,the black sky and the Libra constellation of stars rising in fast motion. Other galactic nebuli and meteor dust were swirling backwards, the red moon was closing in, but maybe it was really a UFO with atomic power pack problems, reverse electromagnetic damage.

Was this happening?

I abandoned all hope. I was sinking into the bed; I was drowning; I was falling. I was being sawed in half like the woman in the box with the magician.

So... this was childbirth? Nobody told me about this part. This wasn't fair. Men didn't have to do this, but they couldn't ever deal with this anyway, men can't stand pain without snapping into idiocy or vegetable-dom.

"What the hell is the deal here?" I yelled at the nurse who walked in eating a ham and swiss on rye and reading *House and Garden*. Mayonnaise was on her weak chin.

"Just calm down, my dear. It'll all be over before you know it. It's not so bad."

"Have you ever done this?" I asked. I needed real sympathy.

"Well, no... but I've seen it thousands of times." The mayonnaise on her chin must have been imitation mayonnaise, because it wasn't melting into her pores. It was just sitting there, getting on my nerves.

"If you've never done this you don't know anything about it. Why don't they hire some nurses who've had children?" I hissed.

"Why don't you try your Lamaze breathing again?"

I was incredulous. I just gaped at her.

"THE LAMAZE METHOD! Are you kidding?!? Don't you think I've already tried that?" At this point the Lamaze Method was about as useful as sandals in a blizzard.

She just looked me over with eyes very dead. Shark attack victims have described shark's eyes that looked like this.

I wanted to escape. I decided to get to the window and jump out to die to end the pain, but the nurse wouldn't let me.

"Lie down," she said, "just lie down."

"This isn't a natural position for childbirth... lying down... I want to squat. Why can't I squat?"

"We can't let you squat?"

"This is really stupid. All I want to do is squat. Women in Africa dig a hole in the ground and squat over it when they're giving birth. The baby comes right out."

"Look, do you want pain medication?" she asked like a heroin dealer, smiling. I remembered that line about the first one being free, which isn't true in real life.

"No. I'm a martyr," I screamed, "can't you see that?" I was not a martyr; I was delirious. I had quit drugs and alcohol for the whole nine months of pregnancy; I hadn't even taken an aspirin; why take something on the last day?

I tried to sit up, roll over, squat, stand in bed, turn, thrash, but she kept holding me down.

"We're going to have to restrain you if you keep trying to move around," she said.

"I can't believe this. What is this place? Dachau?" I screamed. I should have stayed home and had the baby. Friends of mine who had their babies at home were up and active until they felt the baby coming out. Then they just squatted in an easy chair and dropped the baby.

I was so angry I wanted to cry. I held the bridge of my nose the way Marlo Thomas did on the *That Girl* show when she was trying not to cry.

"I'm really thirsty. I haven't had any liquid for twenty four hours," I said. "Can you get me some water?"

"We can't let you have water. Just in case we have to anesthetize you, we don't want anything in your stomach."

I knew all that. They didn't want me to get sick on the anesthesia, and throw up, and have the vomit caught in my esophagus. If only they knew; it took a lot more than a little anesthesia to make me puke.

"Jesus, I have to pee," I said. I did have to pee and while I was in the bathroom I could drink some water from the faucet.

She wouldn't even let me go to the bathroom.

"I have to pee," I screamed. "That's all. Just pee!"

"We can't let you get up," she said. "I'll get you a bed pan. Wait"

While she was out I got up, went to the bathroom and took a piss. I also put my parched lips on the faucet and sucked water, like a person who had been lost in the desert.

The nurse came back. She caught me while I was shuffling back from the bathroom. She was irate.

"I can't believe you got up when I told you NOT TO! Get back in bed and lay down!" She tossed the bedpan aside and handed me a weird oblong yellow thing on a lollipop stick. "This is the only thing you can have before an operation. It'll take your thirst away. Suck on it."

I did.

On this whole planet, there are not too many things eatable or suckable that I cannot easily recognize or give nomenclature to. This yellow thing was one of those things. It was a preoperative horror on a stick, but it was sweet, sort of, so I used it, and it did put some moisture on the tongue. I had been in labor for almost twenty-four hours and I was dry. Anything remotely wet was fine.

When the next contraction came, and the pain was even worse than before, I decided I was dying. Women die in childbirth all the time. I had to think of something else. I forced myself to relax.

Okay. If this was the way it was going to be, then it better be worth it. This kid had better be as formidable as the pain. This kid had better come out of the womb speaking quantum physics, or be telekinetic, or have white hair and purple eyes, or be able to levitate, or have a blue aura, or be the new messiah, or be clutching gold in his little fists, or at least speak like the dolphins speak.

A couple of hours later, he just came out. The head and the shoulders were a push, but the rest of the body just slipped out. It felt like a fish sliding out, like a bloated mackerel.

My baby was a boy and he looked like all the rest of the babies I had seen the day before in the nursery, red and shrivelled and screaming. The umbilical cord looked exactly like a gray coiled telephone wire.

The doctor looked him over. "It's a boy. OH!... but what's this?"

Naturally I panicked. "WHAT'S WRONG WITH HIM!?!"

"Oh... ahh... ahh, it's nothing. I'm sorry... I thought..." The doctor was laughing then. "It's just a birthmark, a black birthmark where he'll never see it in his life... under his scrotum."

There was nothing else weird about him except for his hair. He had the longest, blackest, thickest hair anyone had ever seen at that hospital. And he had a cowlick, ridiculously sticking straight up from nine months of amniotic hair setting. The nurses' aides all went wild about his head of hair. They gave him an Elvis Presley pompadour for his hospital photos. That was something worthwhile.

When the dad saw his son for the first time, he looked pleased, but he told me he was terrified.

I held my kid in my arms when they brought him to me to breast feed. He was like a little monkey, wirey and solid... no fat at all, with strong legs like a mature frog.

I drifted to sleep with him beside me.

"Goodnight, Max," I said to him, "I'm going to sleep now."

I had a dream that Max spoke to me. "It's a good idea to get lots of sleep now, while you have a chance," he suggested in a baritone, "because for many years to come, you're going to need it."

I woke in horror. "I'd better get a Doctor Spock book," I told myself, then I fell asleep again. It was to be the last time I slept soundly for sixteen years.

STAINLESS STEEL REFLECTIONS

by M. J. Canuel

More hours under white lights not knowing
Knowing, my child, two floors above
Waits to be drawn unconscious
Into a cube of stainless steel reflecting
Faces white-masked in anonymity.
I stand in halls echoing generations of antiseptic
While stern starched figures flicker by rushed.
Over my head, there is science and
Caesarean section.
Hinged doors hold fathers at bay
I can hear no pain, no voices, no rite of passage
Just my thudding heart not knowing,
Knowing my child, my dreams will be ushered
Past me, out elevator doors, in a glass box.
Of my body. Of my flesh.

ORAL DISCUSSION

1. What are the similarities and differences between the speakers of these two works?
2. How do the settings differ?
3. Explain the author's tone in each work.
4. Compare and contrast the themes of these two works.

WRITING CHALLENGE

In a comparison and contrast essay, respond to the following statement:

While the essay and the poem in this chapter both deal with the same subject matter, the authors' perspectives are quite different.

The following question now has significance for you.
Add it to the **Writer's Tool Box** at the beginning of your book.

IS MY COMPARISON AND CONTRAST CLEAR AND ORGANIZED?

The Oral Presentation

ORGANIZING

Before You Present

Before giving an oral presentation, you should be thoroughly familiar with what you intend to present. One of the most important aspects of a successful oral presentation is feeling completely comfortable with the subject matter. This means reading, re-reading, viewing, reviewing, listening, re-listening, thinking and rethinking. Doing this will enable you to organize, synthesize, and present information in such a way that it best reflects your personality. The material will then come naturally and easily to you in your presentation.

Getting It Down On Paper

Organizing material for an oral presentation is no different from organizing a written presentation. All the tools you have learned throughout this book can be applied. Your oral presentation must also have an introduction, development and conclusion.

Pacing Your Presentation

Prior to presenting, there are some questions to keep in mind and some decisions to make. Do I want to be speaking for the entire time or do I want to allow the audience time (short pauses) to assimilate what I have said? This can be done through the use of visual aids (charts, acetates, movie clips), special effects (music, quoted passage, rhetorical question). You must be very careful when using any of these because you want them to enhance and not detract from your complete presentation.

Technical Equipment

In addition, you should consider the following. Have I made arrangements to ensure that any technical equipment required will be available and in working order? Am I at ease with the technical equipment I plan on using?

PREPARING

Once you have a written plan of what you want to present, you must decide on how to transpose your ideas from a written to an oral form.

Do Not Read

You may have many words to say but there is no oral presentation worse than one that is a simple reading of a written text. In order to avoid merely reading your text and to ensure that you will have adequately budgeted your presentation time, follow the advice provided below.

Prepare Cue Cards

The cue cards you prepare should contain *the main points* of your presentation. Avoid putting too much information on them. You do not want to find yourself in the situation of scrambling for information while you are presenting.

Rehearse Your Presentation

Practise your oral presentation several times before you actually give it. This will permit you to discover how well you know your material before you are faced with an audience.

Time Yourself

Practise timing yourself. Make sure that you have enough material to present for the time you have been allotted. When you time yourself at home, you should be aware that nervousness tends to speed up the rate at which people speak. Try to speak slowly and clearly enough for the audience to receive the full impact of your presentation.

Visual Aids

If you are using visual aids make sure that your audience will all be able to see what you are showing them and that it is relevant to what you are saying.

Audience Management

You have to decide how you are going to manage your audience. Will you allow for questions during your presentation? Do you want to ask the audience to hold their questions until the end of the presentation? Whatever your decision, you will have to make this clear at the beginning.

Vocabulary

Are there any special terms or vocabulary in your presentation that might require an explanation? If *you* had to look up a word in a dictionary because you were not sure of its meaning, you might want to explain what the word means to your audience.

Getting Comfortable

Are there certain people in your audience that you know well? If there are, make a mental note of where they are sitting so that you can look at them while you present. This will help reduce your anxiety.

PRESENTING

The preparation strategies mentioned above will help to make your presentation more effective. There are, however, certain points to keep in mind during your presentation.

Hold Yourself With Confidence

Be aware of how you are holding yourself. Do you want to stand in the same spot for the whole presentation? Do you want to sit? Do you want to walk around? It has been proven that it is best to vary your positioning during a presentation. Do not move excessively, but allow your audience to move their eyes by varying your positioning from time to time. Let your stance show that you have confidence in yourself and in what you are saying.

Look At Your Audience

Remember to look at your audience. They want to feel involved in your presentation.

Do not Chew Gum

Make sure that the only gum you have is either in your pocket or in the wastebasket.

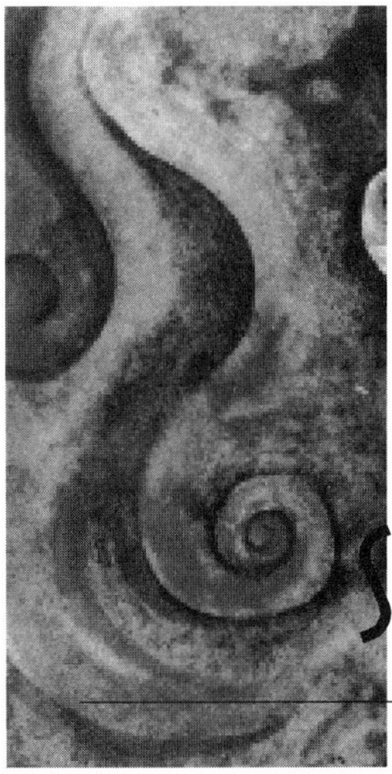

SECTION 1

Subject - Verb Agreement

You may sometimes have difficulty in making subjects and verbs agree. The following hints will help to guide you.

1. When the subject is compound, the verb is plural.

    John and George are here.

2. When the word *there* precedes the verb, the verb agrees with the subject that follows it.

    There are two men here.

3. When the combinations *neither...nor* and *either...or* are used, the verb agrees with the subject that is closer to the verb.

    Neither Pedro nor I want to be here.

    Either their daughters or their son is going to visit us next week.

4. When the subject is separated from the verb by interrupting words like *as well as, in addition to,* the verb agrees with the subject that is usually found before these interrupting words.

    All the employees, as well as their union leader, are here.

5. When the subject is indefinite such as *each, either, neither, everybody, someone, something,* the verb is singular.

    Everybody is here.

6. When the subject is out of its normal position and follows the verb, the verb is singular or plural depending on the subject itself.

    Present at the meeting were Lei and Mikael.

7. Be careful with *who, which, that.* These agree with the subjects that precede them.

    These are the men who live in Timbuktu.

8. Some words look plural but are not, thus you must use a singular verb.

    Mathematics is my major and economics is my brother's major.

CLASS EXERCISE

Proofread the following sentences. Ask yourself the question, *"Do the subject and verb agree in number?"* If the answer is *"No"* correct the problem.

1. An important person in my field of study is Lise Thibodeau, a biologist who specialize in animal physiology.

2. The experiments that Watson did on a little boy, whose name was Albert, was not morally acceptable.

3. Mueller, as well as Selzer and Thurber, have mastered the art of descriptive writing.

4. There was at least two people hurt in the accident.

5. Across the street is a shopping center and a parking lot.

6. I'm not sure whether or not it is Phil or his brothers who wants to go.

7. Physics were one of his favorite subjects.

8. There is a lot of adult students in this college.

9. Standing in front of the crowd was the president and her husband.

10. Everyone in my family have had their fair share of problems, but we all still manage to walk around with smiles on our faces.

EXERCISE 1

Read the following paragraph. If you find an error in subject-verb agreement, correct the error.

Madonna and Bjork are both very popular singers, though their music and their personalities are quite different. Neither of them are old but while Madonna's persona is vampish, Bjork's is more impish. Madonna, with the help of her entourage of managers and advisors, sell an image of sex to women. A lot of the people who likes her music buy into the message that to be a woman in the 1990's means being not only "sexy" but also being in control of your sexuality and using it as a means of getting what you want. A quick look at some of the titles of her songs give proof of this. Her first big hits were "Like a Virgin" and "Respect Yourself," both of which talks about women using sex to get power in relationships. Bjork, on the other hand, is part of a new breed of female singers who uses songs to demonstrate the intellectual power of women. She challenges the typical image of female singers as "sex kittens." Her songs, such as "Isabelle" and "Mama," describes women as complex, three-dimensional beings capable of achieving power through motherhood, intellect, and love. It is rather ironic that even if Bjork's music is the antithesis of Madonna's, Bjork has said in interview after interview that she admires Madonna both as a business person and as an artist.

QUIZ

Proofread the following text and find and correct errors in subject-verb agreement.

Sitting in my living room is two little ugly dolls that my boyfriend, Paul, bought in a little Costa Rican village several years ago. The tribal chief who sold Paul the dolls told him they were voodoo dolls that had been made and used on a couple from a neighboring tribe. After the couple had mysteriously disappeared, the chief decided that the dolls could be sold. I don't like these dolls.

First, they don't exactly blend harmoniously with the decor of our apartment and, second, they give me the creeps. I can't tell you how many arguments has been caused as a result of those dolls. Paul refuses to move them from the living room and I would like to throw them in the fireplace. Since neither of us are ready to change our minds, and since I recognize that Paul really likes those evil creatures (and since he does pays half of the rent) I have decided not to ask that they be moved or destroyed any more. As a result, every time I sit down in the living room, I feel as though those ugly creatures are staring at me and are waiting for an opportunity to attack me.

Now, you might say that everyone know that there is no such thing as voodoo dolls. Well, I agree with you and I'm normally quite skeptical about anything to do with the supernatural. I'm not the type of person who get spooked easily, but that doesn't help me much when it's late at night and I'm alone in my apartment. Paul doesn't know this, but when he's not there I usually throw a towel over the little devils.

> The following question now has significance for you.
> Add it to the **Technical Checklist** at the beginning of your book.
>
> **DO MY SUBJECTS AND VERBS AGREE?**

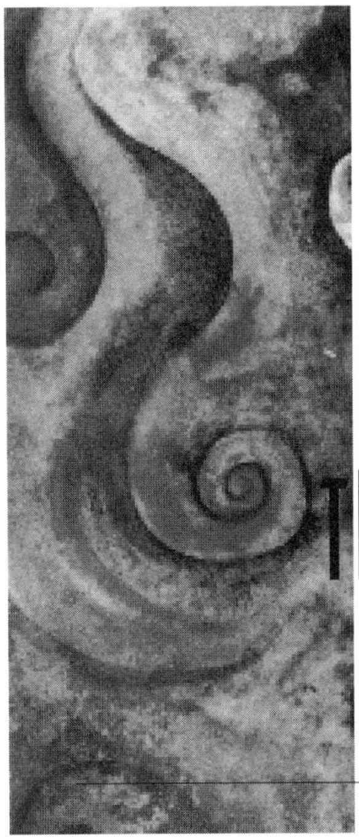

SECTION 2

The Present Perfect Versus The Simple Past

Action at unspecified time in the past. 1.

Action started in the past and continues in the present. 2. X Presssssent Perrrrrrfect →

SIMPLE PAST — PRESENT

Use the PRESENT PERFECT:

- to talk about a completed past action IF you do not know or care when the past action (or actions) occurred

Key words: once, twice, several times, etc.

I've been to Vancouver several times. (Times are not known and not important)

- to talk about an action that began in the past and continues up to the present

Key words: ever, never, up to now, in my whole life, since, for, etc.

I've known Allison since we were in the third grade.

Use the SIMPLE PAST TENSE:

- when an action is over and the time that the action occurred is known

Key words: yesterday, last week, a month ago, last Easter, when I was a child, etc.

Twenty years ago a small child was left on our doorstep.

- if you are telling a story about an event that completely occurred in the past

Once upon a time, a small boy lost his way in the forest. Suddenly a ...

Be careful with the use of *SINCE* and *FOR*. SINCE refers back to a specific time in the past, and FOR refers to a duration of time.

CLASS EXERCISE

Fill in the blanks with either the present perfect or the simple past tense.

I first (*meet*) _______________ (1) my husband in 1968. We (*be*) _______________ (2) at an after school dance called a *sock hop*. Sock hops (*be*) _______________ (3) popular in those days. This type of dance (*get*) _______________ (4) its name in a rather simple way. The students (*be*) _______________ (5) required to remove their shoes before entering the gym. The administration (*ask*) _______________ (6) the students to do this so that the floor wouldn't be scratched.

It's rather strange to realize that I (*know*) _______________ (7) my husband for over twenty-five years. Little did I know that when he (*ask*) _______________ (8) me to dance the first time that we would still be together so many years later. Let me say unequivocally that the relationship (*not, be*) _______________ (9) without its ups and downs. As a matter of fact, we (*have*) _______________ (10) our first fight about two days after the sock hop. I think it (*have*) _______________ (11) something to do with the fact that he had forgotten to break up with girlfriend number 55. By the way, he jokingly (*refer*) _______________ (12) to me as number 56 ever since. I (*tell*) _______________ (13) my husband over and over again that I really resent this particular designation.

The second fight (*happen*) _______________ (14) when we went to a Halloween party.

He had neglected to tell me that it (*be, not*) ______________ ______________ (15) a costume party. I (*arrive*) ______________ (16) decked out in a witch costume—complete with blackened teeth! Number 55 (*be*) ______________ (17) there dressed as her usual gorgeous self. We (*not, dance*) ______________ (18) ; we (*not, talk*) ______________(19); we (*not, leave*) ______________ (20) together. He (*call*) ______________ (21) the next day. We (*be*) ______________ (22) together ever since. We (*not, be*) ______________ (23) to a Halloween party since, and I refuse to play the number 55 in the lottery!

EXERCISE 1

Circle and correct the errors in the following sentences. If the sentence is correct, write "C " beside it.

_____ 1. I have being at school since five o'clock this morning.

_____ 2. Martha went to Austria at least twenty times because her grandmother lives there.

_____ 3. Did you ever eat chocolate-covered ants?

_____ 4. We have studied a lot of grammar since we started this course.

_____ 5. I didn't go to Tibet before, so I'm anxious to see the mountains.

_____ 6. I haven't bought a hot dog from a street vendor since at least fifteen years.

_____ 7. When I was young, I have lived in Tokyo.

_____ 8. I haven't seen Fluffball for several weeks.

_____ 9. Have you ever went to China?

_____ 10. Carol is sometimes such a pain. She didn't even read the book yet, but she already has an opinion about it!

EXERCISE 2

Proofread the following story. Circle and correct any errors.

I went to Florida many times in my life. When I was five years old, my parents have bought a condominium in St. Petersburg while they were visiting my grandparents during the summer. They have bought it because they wanted a place to go every winter when they retired, but I didn't know this. I thought they had bought it so that I would have a place to go every winter. When I have heard that we owned a condo in sunny Florida, I have started to invite all my friends from school. I was the most popular kid in school. Just imagine, I was offering everyone a free vacation! Little did I know that a part of my parents' plan was to rent out the condo to other people for the first few years in order to pay the mortgage on it.

As that first Christmas vacation approached, I was full of anticipation at the prospect of swimming in the ocean after opening all of my presents. I had narrowed my list of potential guests to the four most popular kids at school: Jeff, Harry, Bill, and Eddy. When I went to school, everyone has been very nice to me because they wanted to be part of the elite group that would get to share in my luck. Just imagine my surprise when I have realized that my parents have had no intention of going to Florida that year. I knew that I could never show my face at school again. Needless to say, that was a very friendless Christmas for me.

Since that time, I saw friends come and go, but to this day my parents still have that condo in sunny Florida. I went many times over the years. In fact, I think I'll be going there this year. The moral of the story is that friends may come and go, but real estate is eternal.

QUIZ

Find and correct any errors in subject-verb agreement, and verb tense in the following text. If the sentence is correct, write "C" beside it.

_____ 1. Last week my boss has told me he was firing me because of my incompetence.

_____ 2. I have been sick since last Tuesday when I started to get a cold.

_____ 3. Martine has told Jennifer the verdict last week, and neither of them were surprised with the outcome.

_____ 4. Our college has been founded by the Jesuits in 1967.

_____ 5. Have you ever went to Nepal?

_____ 6. The committee on the future of our local colleges have made its decision at midnight.

_____ 7. Michael, you have received an important call ten minutes ago. Rachid, from Medacorps, want you to call him back.

_____ 8. Once upon a time, Goldilocks has entered the home of three vacationing bears.

_____ 9. Although all my friends smoke, I never tried it because I watched my father die from lung cancer when I was a child.

_____ 10. We have become colleagues in 1994 when we began to work together.

The following question now has significance for you.
Add it to the **Technical Checklist** at the beginning of your book.

AM I USING THE PRESENT PERFECT TENSE CORRECTLY?

SECTION 3

The Past Perfect Versus The Simple Past

The **PAST PERFECT** is the past of the past. If you are writing in the past, you use the past perfect to indicate that an action or event occurred *BEFORE* another past time action.

Last night the dog was picked up by the dog pound because it had bitten too many people.

PAST PERFECT — SIMPLE PAST — PRESENT

—X—X—X——X-X———————! ———————! ————→

the dog had bitten too many people — *the dog was picked up*

* If the situation begins in the present, use the simple past not the past perfect.

Examples:

*The fridge **is** empty.*	*The family **has** already **eaten**.*
*The fridge **was** empty.*	*The family **had** already **eaten**.*

CLASS EXERCISE

Complete the sentences with the words in parentheses. Use the present perfect tense, the simple past tense or the past perfect tense.

1. Rajiv doesn't want to watch that movie with us. He (*see*) ______________________________ it.

2. Natalia didn't want to watch the movie with us last night. She (*see*) _________________________ it.

3. Last summer I (*go*) ______________________________ across the country. I (*drive*) ______________________________ from Montreal to Vancouver. I was very excited about seeing Vancouver because I (*never, be*) ______________________________ before. I (*spend*) ______________________________ several days staying at a hotel near the beach. Before that trip, I (*never, see*) ______________________________ the ocean before.

4. Mark (*be*) ______________________________ late for our date last Friday night. He (*apologize*) ______________________________ to me, and explained that the police (*stop*) ______________________________ him on his way to the theater.

5. My bachelor son (*invite*) ______________________________ me to dinner several weeks ago. He (*serve*) ______________________________ potato chips and soft drinks because he thought that I (*offer*) ______________________________ to bring dinner with me!

EXERCISE 1

Proofread the following paragraphs. Circle and correct the tense errors.

1. Last Friday, when I arrived at the club, Marco was waiting for me at the bar. He was waiting for awhile and he was, unfortunately, quite upset. I explained to him that I forget at which club we were supposed to meet. Marco sat sullenly and refused to even talk to me. When I suggested that we begin our tennis match, he told me that he al-

ready play a game with someone else. I then made the mistake of telling Marco that he was acting childish. I realized that I kept Marco waiting at the club for a long time because he was in no mood to forgive me for my tardiness. He picked up his towel and tennis racket, and without so much as a nod, he stomped out of the club. I didn't speak to him since then.

2. Yesterday my friend, Midge, was late for work. She came flying into the office around 11 a.m., her face flushed and her hair in disarray because she knew that she missed a 9 a.m. appointment with a client. We were ready to tease her about it when she explained to all of us that she had an accident. Fortunately, our boss, Mr. Bean, wasn't angry because he already heard about the accident. Midge's boyfriend called earlier that morning and explained the situation.

QUIZ

Proofread the following paragraph and correct any errors in subject-verb agreement and verb tense.

On October 23, 1987, I found myself in London, England with no money, no friends and no umbrella to shelter me from the pouring rain. I arrived in England two weeks earlier for a little rest and relaxation. I had worked hard over the previous summer in order to save enough money to afford the trip. My parents even gave me some money! What I hadn't realize is that London is a very expensive city. By the end of the first week of my trip, I already spent almost all my money. That October 23 morning, I have decided to call my family in Canada to ask for more money. However, neither my parents nor my older brother were there. They left for a vacation of their own a week earlier. So, I found myself in London without so much as two nickels to rub together. As a result, after my phone call, I had gone to the British Airways office to see if I could get an earlier flight home. Luckily, there was a seat available since someone had canceled the previous evening. When I had gotten home, I felt like kissing the ground. The moral of this story, as well as millions of others like it, are that when you travel, don't leave home without a credit card.

The following question now has significance for you.
Add it to the **Technical Checklist** at the beginning of your book.

HAVE I CORRECTLY USED THE PAST PERFECT TENSE?

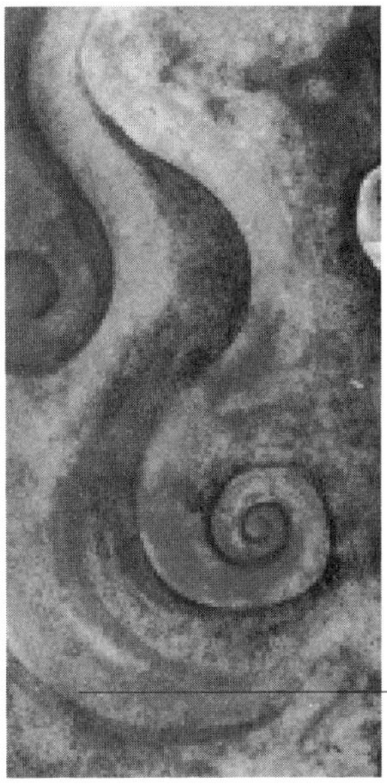

SECTION 4

Pronoun Pitfalls

Even advanced students sometimes use the incorrect **pronoun form**. Look at the following: *Ms. Lau is the personal assistant to the president, Ms. Kalenko.* ***She*** *is very easy to work with.* Shortcuts can get a writer into trouble. For example, it is unclear whether the pronoun *she* refers to Ms. Lau or Ms. Kalenko. Listed below are some common pronoun pitfalls.

Refer to the chart below when you need to choose the correct pronoun form.

PRONOUN FORMS

Subject	*Object*	*Reflexive*	*Possessive*	*Possessive Adjectives*
I	me	myself	mine	my
you	you	yourself	yours	your
he	him	himself	his	his
she	her	herself	hers	her
it	it	itself		its
we	us	ourselves	ours	our
you	you	yourselves	yours	your
they	them	themselves	theirs	their

The following hints will help you decide which pronoun form to use.

1. When two nouns are joined by *OR* or *NOR*, the pronoun should agree with the nearest noun.

   Either Susan or Elizabeth will have to lend me ***her*** *book.*

   Neither Helen nor the Greens want to give up ***their*** *course.*

2. When the pronoun is a part of a **compound subject**, use the **subject pronoun**.

   The manager and ***I*** *had a meeting together.*

3. Use **object pronouns** in these cases:

   a) when the pronoun is the **direct** or **indirect object** of the verb.

   The general manager gave Mr. Ellis and ***me*** *tickets for the ball game.*

   Who gave the tickets? ______________

   Who received the tickets? ______________

Asking yourself these types of questions will tell you the *subject* of the sentence (doer of the action) as well as the *object* of the sentence (receiver of the action). After this, it is easy to decide whether you need to use a subject or object pronoun.

   b) when the pronoun is the object of a preposition.

   Between *you and me, that answer was unclear.*

   The gift is ***for*** *her and not for me.*

   c) after an infinitive.

   Josh wanted the winner ***to be*** *her.*

   Alan was supposed ***to call*** *me.*

4. Use **reflexive pronouns** when the subject doing the action and the object receiving the action are the same.

   The Smiths should help ***themselves*** *to the coffee.*

   He is very proud of ***himself****.*

5. Sometimes a pronoun appears at the end of the sentence, and you may not be sure if you should use the subject or the object pronoun. When in doubt, *complete the thought.*

   *She has worked here longer than (**I** / me).*

   She has worked here longer ***than I have****.*

*The car belongs to Jane as much as (I / **me**).*

*The car belongs to Jane as much as **it belongs to me**.*

6. Be sure that you know the differences in meaning of the following groups of words. THEIR, THERE AND THEY'RE; YOUR and YOU'RE; and ITS and IT'S. The first one in the group is the **possessive adjective** in each case.

7. Avoid using **personal pronouns** (I, you, we) in literary criticism.

   ***You** will notice that the climax occurs when the meat is eaten.*

   This could be changed to:

   The climax occurs when the meat is eaten.

CLASS EXERCISE

Put the correct answer in the space provided.

1. _______ and her boyfriend were planning a big wedding. (*She* / *Her*)
2. This is a secret between you and _______. (*me* / *I*)
3. Jasmine told her husband that she is just as smart as _______. (*he* / *him*)
4. Carol wanted us to play, but Alice and _______ were not really interested. (*me* / *I*)
5. Strictly between you and _______, I don't like him. (*I* / *me*)
6. Last year, after my wedding, _______ and his sister visited me. (*him* / *he*)
7. This matter concerns you as much as _______. (*me* / *I*)
8. _______ and her father were going on a fishing trip. (*She* / *Her*)
9. Anne asked us to visit, but Joe and _______ couldn't make it. (*me* / *I*)
10. A month ago _______ and his friend were in Miami. (*he* / *him*)

EXERCISE 1

Proofread the following text. Circle and correct the pronoun errors.

I'm very proud of me because I have just successfully completed an apprenticeship in a large multinational company. Nobody in my program thought that I was the best person for this particular challenge and many thought that they were far more qualified than me. For a time, I thought that my peers were correct in there assessment. For example, one of my schoolmates thought that I'd make a fool of me. Before making such ridiculous comments, he should have taken a good look at hisself in the mirror. He seemed to be under the impression that he was smarter than me, just because he had received better marks in school than me. Both him and I did our apprenticeship in the same company, and it was me, not him, that was offered a job. He may still think he is better than me, but I'll let the facts speak for theirselves.

A **pronoun shift** occurs when the pronoun and its antecedent do not agree.
Example:

Every student *should do* ***their*** *best.* ***Every student*** *should do* ***his*** *or* ***her*** *best*

* Remember to use a singular pronoun when referring to *anyone / someone / everyone / or anyone.*
* To avoid having to assign gender, it is preferable to use a plural noun.

For example, the sentence above could be corrected to read:

Students should do ***their*** *best.*

EXERCISE 2

The following sentences have errors in: *pronoun usage* and *pronoun shift.* Circle the errors and write the correct form in the space provided. If the sentence is correct, write "C" in the space provided.

_______ 1. Every worker should try their hardest.

_______ 2. After her strange reaction, I asked me if I had been rude.

_______ 3. People should act respectfully towards your hosts.

_______ 4. Our friends helped themselves to the punch.

_______ 5. She is under the mistaken impression that she can type better than me.

_______ 6. If anyone is hungry, they can have a sandwich.

_______ 7. At that school, students must pay according to how many courses you take.

_______ 8. Every child should discuss this issue with their parents.

_______ 9. When your young, you don't have a lot of experience.

_______ 10. Anne can bake as well as me.

PRONOUN QUIZ

Correct the errors of pronoun usage in the following text.

My best friend Ted and me have to discuss something. He claims that I don't really listen to he and his friends. He even accuses me of not respecting them. His accusation is clearly ridiculous, but I'll let you readers judge for yourself. To prove his point, Ted refers to the time that me and him went to a club with his friend Peter. He says that I ignored Peter. Now I'll grant you that Peter and me didn't have an earth-shattering conversation, but then it's rather difficult to carry on a conversation with someone who keeps his eyes on a TV screen in the corner of the room. Peter can talk for hours about some silly trade that the Calgary Flames made. BORING. But it's clearly overstating the case to say that I was rude! That is really a ridiculous complaint. Ted is much ruder than me, although he'd probably tell you that I'm ruder than him.

That same night at that same club, Ted struck up a conversation with a woman at the next table, and he ignored both Peter and I. Whenever I tried to get Ted's attention, he shooed me away like a pesky fly. And to top it off, Ted and Peter helped theirselves to my french fries. I swear I had to fight for a few measly fries! If they'd really wanted fries, they could have ordered some for theirselves! Now maybe your going to say that the three of us sound childish, and you could be right. Perhaps Ted and I should bury the hatchet, and I should realize that both him and me were equally rude. You could say that I was as impolite as him.

The following question now has significance for you.
Add it to the **Technical Checklist** at the beginning of your book.

HAVE I AVOIDED THE PRONOUN PITFALLS?

SECTION 5

Punctuating to Avoid Fragments and Run-Ons

Fragments are *incomplete* and can very often fool writers because they look like complete sentences.

Remember a complete sentence must:

- have a subject
- have a complete verb
- express a complete thought

For example, the following are considered fragments as they are not complete sentences:

- *One day last November had an accident.* (This has no subject.)
- *Vanessa leaving the room.* (This has an incomplete verb; the auxiliary is missing.)
- *When I was fired.* (Although there is both a subject and a verb, the sentence on its own is meaningless.)

Run-on sentences are composed of two or more sentences strung together without any appropriate connection. Run-on sentences can also fool a writer because they contain too many subjects, verbs and complete thoughts.

For example, the following is a run-on sentence:

Olivia started college in 1986 she finally graduated in 1995.

(This sentence has two subjects-*Olivia* and *she*. It has two verbs-*started* and *graduated*. It expresses two completely different thoughts.)

CLASS EXERCISE

Read each of the following and decide if it is a fragment (**F**), a run on (**RO**), or complete (**C**).

_______ 1. Because there was a lot of traffic.

_______ 2. Many car owners are learning to do their own repairs they find this significantly less expensive.

_______ 3. After spilling the pasta on the floor and trying to clean it up with a wad of Kleenex.

_______ 4. The sun had risen the sky was an azure blue the birds were singing a cheerful tune and I was ready for a dip in the ocean.

_______ 5. There are many way to solve her problems, and I am willing to help as much as I can.

_______ 6. Once I am able to sort out all of the intricacies of English grammar.

USING COMMAS AND SEMICOLONS

The last exercise showed you how to spot two common sentence faults: fragments and run-ons. While it is essential to be able to spot a fragment or a run-on, you must have the appropriate strategies to effectively eliminate them. Correct use of the comma and semicolon will help you to do this.

USING THE COMMA

1. Use a comma before *and, but, for, or, nor, yet and so* when any of these is used to connect **independent clauses** (short, complete sentences) in a **compound sentence** (long sentence composed of two or more complete sentences).

   *Olivia started college in 1986, and she finally graduated in 1995.**

   * In the above example, a comma is used before the conjunction. Most grammarians agree that in this case the comma is optional because the sentence is short. In your own writing, if you are not sure whether or not to use a comma in a compound sentence, you should use one. Doing this will allow you confidence in punctuating. At all costs avoid the "salt and pepper" method of sprinkling a few commas here and there to simply make your work "look punctuated."

2. Use a comma after an introductory statement.

   After I ate, I put my dishes in the dishwasher.

   In spite of all her effort, she will fail the course.

3. Use commas to separate items in a series. Note that a series is composed of three or more words.

   Joshua packed his blue sweater, brown pants, red shirt, and yellow socks.

4. Use commas to separate any component in a sentence that contains information that is not essential to the meaning of the sentence. Pay special attention to *who, which, that* clauses.

   My mother, who is an orthodontist, lives in Thunder Bay.

5. Use commas to separate words or expressions such as *moreover, however, of course, in my opinion, incidentally, thus, therefore* that interrupt the main flow of the sentence and are not essential to the meaning of the sentence.

   I do, however, have another complaint.

6. Use a comma(s) in dates and place names.

   I was born on July 12, 1964, in Chatham, Ontario.

USING THE SEMICOLON

1. Use a semicolon to join two complete sentences that have no other connector.

   Olivia started college in 1986; she finally graduated in 1995.

2. Use a semicolon before any of the following transitional words when they are used in a compound sentence: *accordingly, besides, consequently, finally, furthermore, however, incidentally, indeed, meanwhile, moreover, nevertheless, otherwise, therefore, thus.* Note that each of these transitional words is followed by a comma.

   The mall was closed; consequently, we went to the corner store.

3. Use semicolons to separate items in a series if these items already contain commas.

   Josie showed us the pictures of her trip to Montreal, Quebec; Ottawa, Ontario; Charlottetown, Prince Edward Island; and Fredricton, New Brunswick.

CLASS EXERCISE

Correct the following sentences, if necessary. If the sentence is already correct, write "C" in the space provided.

_______ 1. I chose to go to bed early last night and not watch the news. Because I was tired after having worked for twelve hours.

_______ 2. There were several students who were late with their reports this was unacceptable.

_______ 3. I am due to return to work in two days; so I might as well make the best of what's left of my vacation and stay in bed until noon.

_______ 4. When I saw her, I couldn't believe my eyes, she had aged a great deal.

_______ 5. Roger, Jeremy, Luke and Simon, are working as accounting clerks in Toronto.

_______ 6. There will be at least five hundred late registrations this semester, this will make it very difficult to complete the students' schedules on time.

EXERCISE 1

Proofread the following paragraph carefully. Eliminate any fragments or run ons. Add any missing commas or semicolons.

Every year many Canadians visit Disney World in Orlando Florida. Many of these visitors fly to Florida some endure a twenty-four hour car ride. No matter how they travel. They all share that desire to see Mickey himself in person. Most visitors are amazed with the facilities. That awe and impress. The colors and sounds are vibrant and exciting children shout and giggle with glee. Parents on the other hand are somewhat daunted by the lengthy lines and American dollar exchange. Which fluctuates daily. Yes Disney World is an American icon that continues to grow in popularity a visit has almost become a rite of passage for many North American children. Just ask a group of eight year olds where they would like to spend a week's vacation they are sure to answer Disney World.

QUIZ

Proofread the following paragraph. Correct any errors in subject-verb agreement, verb tense, pronouns and sentence formation.

I have traveled throughout many countries on this planet. I've went to Istanbul, Turkey, Benares, India, Alor Star, Malaysia, Osaka, Japan, Athens, Greece, and Macon, France. Some people travel to explore other worlds, others moves constantly because they want to run away from themselfes. If I could describe what it was that made me spend so many years on the road. I could only call it something like an addiction to new sensations.

Whenever a place began to feel stale or mundane to me I packed my bags and headed on to a new city. I found me feeling very self-confident and sure of myself when I arrived in new towns. Because people didn't know who I was, and weren't necessarily going to know who I would be in the future. I felt extremely free to be myself; to be open, and to be exceptionally honest with strangers. I also developed the ability to look a stranger in the eye; to smile and to engage them in conversations that had some depth and meaning. Most important of all, the fact that my senses were constantly being stimulated with new and beautiful sights. This made me feel extremely alive.

Rather than worry about my work schedule, or about some floundering relationship; my life on the road was one of acute "living in the present." The colors of buildings; the sounds of people being called to prayer; and the smiles and chatter of hundreds of new faces kept my senses constantly stimulated and aroused. I had felt like I was experiencing life, and not merely passing through it. However I knew that one day I would have to stop moving, settle down in one place, and create a home for myself. With more lasting relationships to both the people and the place.

The following questions now have significance for you.
Add them to the **Technical Checklist** at the beginning of your book.

ARE MY SENTENCES COMPLETE? ARE THEY PUNCTUATED CORRECTLY?

SECTION 6

Using Quotation Marks and Citing References

It is sometimes tricky to decide how to punctuate when using quotation marks. The following rules will help you.

1. Capitalize the first word to the right of the quotation marks *only* if it is the first word of a sentence.

   *Mary said, "**You've** arrived just in time."*

   If the first word in quotations is not the first word in the sentence, do not capitalize it.

   *"You've arrived just in time," said Mary, "**because** I need you."*

2. If the quotation comes before the speaker identification, put a comma to the left of the quotation marks.

   *"You've arrived just in time**,**" said Mary.*

3. If the speaker identification comes before the quotation, put a comma to the left of the quotation marks.

   *Mary said**,** "You've arrived just in time."*

4. Periods *always* go inside quotation marks.

5. If the quotation itself is a question put the question mark inside the quotation marks.

   *"Do you know why I'm here**?**" asked George.*

6. Remember to change paragraphs each time the speaker changes.

CLASS EXERCISE

Complete the following by adding appropriate quotation marks and end punctuation where necessary.

The Polo shirts are on sale at The Bay said my sister-in-law and Jason would really like one for Christmas. This was my motivation for being in the shopping center parking lot three weeks before Christmas. Cars were darting in and out, and the atmosphere was frenzied. I'm the type of person who hates to park far from a mall entrance, and so I was really glad to see the perfect spot about ten feet away. What I didn't see was the free-standing cement post. All I heard was the crunch of grinding metal. The car wouldn't budge, and the left front wheel was stuck up on the pillar.

Lady, you'd better not back up. You're stuck. Jammed up real solid

Have you got a jack asked another passerby

I hope you know you probably bent the frame offered one Japanese gentleman in a tone that suggested that smashing a Honda was tantamount to insulting the entire Japanese nation.

How the heck did you do that asked another

Women drivers! sneered his friend.

You did what gasped my husband at the other end of the cellular.

I called the police, and they're sending a patrol car and a tow truck I wailed. My hands were shaking and my feet were freezing. Needless to say I hadn't followed that age old Boy Scout adage be prepared.

Two hours and several hundred comments later, the tow truck arrived. By this time every person from the ages of five to seventy-five had taken their potshot at the crazy blond lady who had managed to drive her husband's car up onto a cement post.

Don't worry we'll have you down in a couple of minutes explained the tow truck driver who looked about ten years old. I couldn't look as the car was lifted and eased from its cement prison. I suppose I should mention that I had managed to leave the tow truck driver very little room to maneuver, and as he backed, up his back fender hit the cement post and missed being stuck by a hair.

The shirts are on sale until next Saturday, and I'll make sure that I take my own car this time. On the other hand, I may not bother going at all since the $250 deductible for the car repair has already made the sale price irrelevant.

Below are some helpful hints for punctuating titles correctly:

1. Most words in a title are capitalized. Normally, **articles** (a, an, the) and **connecting words** (prepositions and conjunctions) are not capitalized unless they are the first word in the title or come after a colon. This rule can be broken if it is for a specific reason. For example, in the title *A Concise Guide to Love, Marriage* ***And*** *Divorce*, the writer capitalizes the word *And* to emphasize it.

2. Quotation marks are used when short poems, short stories, essays, magazine or newspaper articles are referred to in writing because they are too short to be published as separate entities.

   I really enjoyed "The Dog that Bit People," by James Thurber.

3. Use single quotation marks for a quotation or a short title enclosed in quotation marks.

   Evangalista said, "I read 'Do not Go Gentle into that Good Night' in my English class."

4. If you are dealing with a longer work, such as a book, a play, a movie, a painting, a long poem or a periodical, that was published as a separate entity, you can identify it by underlining the title of the work (when writing by hand) or by using italics (when typing it).

   Leonardo Da Vinci's <u>Mona Lisa</u> is considered to be his masterpiece. *OR*
   Leonardo Da Vinci's *Mona Lisa* is considered to be his masterpiece.

CLASS EXERCISE

Correct the errors in the following sentences.

1. Most agents agree that Casablanca is among the best movies ever made.
2. Catcher in the Rye is a book that appeals to all ages.
3. There are few songs that have the popular appeal of Stairway to Heaven, by Led Zeppelin.
4. The Broadway play applause is based on the movie All About Eve.
5. Discus Thrower is one of the essays included in the book, Reading for the Write Reasons.

QUOTING FROM AN OUTSIDE SOURCE

Whenever you quote directly from another source, you have to let the reader know that the words you are using belong to someone else. This can be done in two ways:

1. If the quote is less than three lines (or less than approximately forty words), you can include the quote as part of your text.

   The best use of description in the short story, "The Birth of Max Mueller-September 25, 1971," is when the author writes, "He had the longest, blackest, thickest hair anyone had ever seen at that hospital. And he had a cowlick, ridiculously sticking straight up from nine months of amniotic hair setting." This example clearly demonstrates Mueller's excellent turn of phrase.

2. If the quote takes more than three lines (approximately forty words or more), you should write it apart from the rest of the text. Since the quote is separate from the rest of the text, quotation marks are not necessary.

   *The following statement has been made by one student of literature:**

   > *There are far too many rules for writing in English. There are verb-tense rules, punctuation rules, and even rules for quoting outside sources.*
   >
   > *Perhaps this is the reason why it is so difficult to write good essays. If it were up to me, I would speak rather than write.*

   It is evident that while most students find the rules for writing difficult, it is these same rules that help them to become better writers.

* NOTE that a colon is used in the above example to introduce the long quotation. Use a colon *only after* a complete sentence to introduce a long quotation, an example or a list.

  Before leaving for your hike, you should make sure that you have each of the following: comfortable shoes, a warm jacket, a hat, and matches.

If you are quoting directly from an outside source, as was done above, you have to give the quoted author credit for his or her words. Even if you do not quote the author directly, but paraphrase or even use one of his or her ideas in your text, you must indicate where you got the information from. Failure to do this results in **plagiarism** which is perhaps the worst crime an academic can commit. There are several acceptable referencing styles depending on the type of writing you are doing. The most popular style for literary analysis is the MLA (Modern Language Association of America) style.

CITING REFERENCES

1. When you include a quote in your text, you can cite the source (or reference) from which you found the quote by writing the author's name and the page number where you found the quote in parentheses.

   The best use of description in the short story, "The Birth of Max Mueller-September 25, 1971," (Mueller 69) is when the author writes, "He had the longest, blackest, thickest hair anyone had ever seen at that hospital. And he had a cowlick, ridiculously sticking straight up from nine months of amniotic hair setting." This example clearly demonstrates Mueller's excellent turn of phrase.

2. If you borrow an idea from an author or if you paraphrase an author, you still have to indicate the source from which you got the information by writing the author's name and the page number where you found the information.

   Plagiarism is considered to be one of the worst academic crimes any student can commit (Aziz-Canuel, Gaetz, and Pawsey 134). If there are more than three authors, you only need to indicate the first author's name followed by et al. For example - (Dion, et al. 33).

HOW TO ORGANIZE A REFERENCE PAGE

Once you have told the reader where you got your information from, you must then make a bibliographic reference for the citation. The bibliography goes at the end of your text (in alphabetical order of the author's name) and gives detailed information so that the reader can verify the information for him or herself.

Works Cited (this is the title for your bibliographic reference page)

All references should appear in alphabetical order. This first reference is from a book so you would cite it as follows:

Aziz-Canuel, Donna, Lynne Gaetz, and Richard Pawsey. *Reading for the Write Reasons*. Scarborough, ON: Prentice Hall Canada, 1997.

This second reference is an essay that is a part of a collection in a longer work so you would cite it as follows:

Mueller, Cookie. "The Birth of Max Mueller — September 25, 1971." *Reading for the Write Reasons*. Donna Aziz-Canuel, Lynne Gaetz, and Richard Pawsey. Scarborough, ON: Prentice Hall Canada, 1997.

These two samples are representative of the type of references that you will be using in literary analysis. This list is by no means an exhaustive one as there are many different rules for particular types of citations. A complete list can be found in the *MLA Handbook for Writers of Research Papers* (New York: Modern Language Association of America, 1988).

It is not necessary to memorize the rules for referencing. Instead, you should have a reference guide close at hand that you can refer to when the need arises.

The following questions now have significance for you.
Add them to the **Technical Checklist** at the beginning of your book.

HAVE I USED QUOTATION MARKS CORRECTLY?
HAVE I CITED REFERENCES CORRECTLY?

SECTION 7

Sentence Problems

Good writing requires that you use a variety of sentence types. Look at the following types of sentences:

* **simple sentence** – one independent clause

My favorite movie is ***Murder on the Orient Express.***

* **compound sentence** – two or more independent clauses

The weather was terrible, so we canceled the trip.

* **complex sentence** – one independent clause and one or more dependent clauses

Marietta, whom I usually admire, received plenty of credit for the play, but she didn't share the accolades with the rest of the cast.

You have probably realized that the more complicated the sentence the greater the chances of error. Several types of sentence error are **misplaced modifiers**, **dangling modifiers**, **ambiguity** and **lack of parallel structure**. Being able to recognize these types of errors is the first step in eliminating them.

Misplaced Modifiers A misplaced modifier is a word or group of words which has been incorrectly placed. The result of this misplacement is either humor or confusion. Either result is unsatisfactory since the reader's attention is diverted from what you are saying.

Wanted: Mother's helper to care for child that does not smoke.

This sentence could be corrected by changing the placement of the modifier "that does not smoke."

Wanted: non-smoking mother's helper.

Dangling Modifiers A dangling modifier is a word or group of words that has no clear connection with the word or group of words it is intended to modify. The result is again confusion and/or humor, both of which are unsatisfactory.

One of the crystal wine glasses fell and broke while polishing the cabinet.

This sentence could not be corrected by shifting the position of the modifier "polishing the cabinet." The entire sentence would have to be edited. One possibility would be:

One of the crystal wine glasses fell and broke while I was polishing the cabinet.

CLASS EXERCISE

Read the following. Identify and correct any misplaced or dangling modifiers.

Working as a magazine editor has been the fulfillment of one of my life's dreams. One of my biggest challenges was the editing of a manuscript written by a former politician. He left his personal papers to the public domain after he quit politics for the benefit of future historians. Browsing through these documents, an article on displaced people caught my eye. The article described how he had been responsible for a debate on a bill to provide help for the homeless in parliament. I promptly notified my direct superior that I was onto an article that showed a particularly human side of this politician's personality. The piece was well-written, informative, and was sure to make a difference in the public's perception of this notoriously selfish politician. Accustomed to reading manuscripts by authors that were badly written, this piece was a special find.

Ambiguity A word or expression is ambiguous when it has two or more potential meanings. This type of faulty construction is confusing for the reader and difficult for the writer to spot.

Bianca did not care for Mick.

Ambiguity is often a result of misplaced modifiers, faulty pronoun reference or incorrect syntax. Whatever the reason, the end result is confusion: an undesired effect of any writing sample. In the example, we do not know if *Bianca disliked Mick* or if *Bianca did not take care of Mick.*

One suggestion that will help you eliminate ambiguity is to put your rough copy aside for a few hours (or a few minutes in the case of a writing exam) and to return with a fresh *proof-reading eye.* You can then try to eliminate any ambiguity errors by:

- using the dictionary to check for multiple meanings of an ambiguous word or expression

  He prefers eggs over toast.

- altering the punctuation of the sentence

  The runner who had been training hurriedly entered the room.

- checking the use of pronouns

  Miran really wants to try sailing although he has never been on one.

CLASS EXERCISE

Read each of the following sentences and try to find the errors in ambiguity. Correct them as necessary. Answers will vary.

1. This office will be open to workers only from nine to five.
2. Stolen necklace found by van.
3. Athletes who are afraid to fly frequently take the train.
4. The party was held on the same night as the concert, so we had to miss it.
5. How will they find the house next time?

Parallel Structure When any number of items are presented in a series, each item must take the same form. Failure to do this results in awkwardness.

One day the man disappeared stealing two thousand dollars in cash and pilfered several hand tools.

This sentence is lacking in parallel structure. The word " pilfered" must be replaced with "pilfering" to achieve parallel structure.

One day the man disappeared stealing two thousand dollars in cash and pilfering several hand tools.

1 **2** **3** **4**

Any meal should be simple, something nutritious, and nicely presented and easily prepared.

This sentence is also lacking in parallel structure. The four items in the list must be put into the same grammatical form.

Any meal should be simple, nutritious, nicely presented and easily prepared.

CLASS EXERCISE

Read the following paragraph. Correct errors in misplaced modifiers, dangling modifiers, ambiguity and parallel structure.

1. People have regretted their lives and wanting something more for as long as man has existed.
2. My secretary's job consists of opening the mail, filing it, screening phone calls, and to oversee the petty cash.
3. The doctor has diagnosed her problem as twofold: psychological and physiology.
4. Some teenagers are dependent on their parents to see that they make their lunches, getting up on time, and do their homework assignments.
5. A person can always get a loan at the bank if you have a good credit rating.

QUIZ

Read the following paragraph. Correct errors in misplaced modifiers, dangling modifiers, ambiguity and parallel structure.

There seems to be a North American fascination with coffee that continues to grow yearly. Most major metropolitan cities are home to a variety of "coffee bars." Within their walls, one is able to find patrons drinking dozens of coffee combinations whose names are sometimes many words in length. It is not unusual to hear a patron asking for, "A double espresso to go." What is the fascination with these places? Are they representative of the ever-burgeoning notion of neighborhood? These establishments are usually perceived as warm and exciting venues where conversation is promoted. Is it indicative of people's reluctance to patronize traditional bars? Certainly coffee is a more economical beverage than drinking beer. Are they a reflection of what North American media present as the *in* place to frequent? The most popular sitcoms on television: "Friends," "Ellen," and "Frasier" regularly portray their characters ordering and sipping a variety of coffee beverages made by designers. Whatever the reasons, these establishments seem sure to become a part of any and all milieus. Maybe North America is ready to shift their loyalty from "Bud Light" to "Juan Valdez."

The following question now has significance for you.
Add it to the **Technical Checklist** at the beginning of your book.

HAVE I CHECKED MY WRITING FOR:

- **misplaced modifiers?**
- **dangling modifiers?**
- **ambiguity?**
- **parallel structure?**

SECTION 8

Spelling Pitfalls

There are many types of spelling errors that even native English speakers make. When you are writing your rough copy, get your ideas down, and during the revision phase of your writing, you can then look carefully at spelling.

SPELLING HINTS

Try keeping a spelling log. Every time you make a spelling error, record the correct spelling form in your notebook. Keep this notebook handy when you are writing.

Using a dictionary or *spell check* function when editing is also a good idea. If you are not sure how to spell something, remember to look up the **base word** in the dictionary. Be aware that spell check has its limits. It will only find misspelled words, but not misused words. For example: *their* or *there* used incorrectly would not be found.

SPELLING HINTS FOR COMMON PREFIXES

- When the **prefix** ends with the same consonant as the base word, make sure that both consonants are kept.

  il + legal = illegal   *un + necessary = unnecessary*

- When the prefix ends with *a* or *i* and the base word begins with the same letter, you should usually use a hyphen after the prefix.

  semi-independent   *anti-intellectual*

- When the prefix ends with *e* or *o* and the base word starts with the same letter, you usually, but not always, omit the hyphen.

  coordinate   *reelect*   *co-owner*

CLASS EXERCISE

Here is a list of common prefixes with their meanings. Brainstorm, and write examples of words next to each prefix. The first word is shown as an example.

a (*not*)	*amoral*	il (*not*)	________
ante (*before*)	________	in (*not*)	________
anti (*against*)	________	im (*not*)	________
bi (*two*)	________	inter (*between*)	________
circum (*around*)	________	mal (*bad*)	________
co (*together*)	________	mis (wrong)	________
col (*with*)	________	multi (*many*)	________
com (*together*)	________	non (*not*)	________
contra (*opposite*)	________	pre (*before*)	________
dis (*not*)	________	re (*again*)	________
en (*give, make*)	________	semi (*half*)	________
ex (*former*)	________	trans (*across*)	________
extra (*out*)	________	tri (*three*)	________
fore (*before*)	________	un (*not*)	________
hyper (*excessive*)	________		

SPELLING HINTS FOR COMMON SUFFIXES

- The final *e* on words should be dropped when adding a **suffix** that begins with a vowel.

  sense – sensible *sincere – sincerity*

- The final *ce* or *ge* should be kept when adding a suffix that begins with *a* or *o*.

  change – changeable *courage – courageous*

If the suffix begins with *i*, the *e* is usually dropped.

finance – financial

- If the base word ends in a *consonant - y*, change the *y* to *i* (unless the suffix begins with *i*)

  Italy + an = Italian *ordinary + ly = ordinarily*

  thirty + ish = thirtyish *lobby + ist = lobbyist*

CLASS EXERCISE

Create words by adding these common suffixes. The first word is shown as an example.

Group 1 ***To form nouns from verbs***

______*revision*	______ing
______sion	______y
______ment	______er
______ation	______or
______al	______ure
______ance	______th

Group 2 ***To form verbs from (a) nouns***

______ate	______ize

(b) from adjectives

______ify	______en

Group 3 ***To form adjectives (a) from nouns***

______ly	______ic
______ful	______less
______al	______ous

(b) from verbs

______ed *	______able
______ing *	______ive
______ant	______ent

* Note the difference : He is *boring*. (*boring* describes what type of person he is)

He is *bored*. (*bored* describes his state of mind)

EXERCISE 1

Choose the correct words from the list provided in each sentence. Use a dictionary if needed.

1. *(lose / loose / loss)*

   I didn't ______________ my new shirt. I gave it away because it was too ______________.

   In any case, I never even liked the shirt so giving it away was no great ______________.

2. *(accept / except)*

   I understand and ______________ everything that you've said ______________ for your last comment. You went a little too far with that complaint.

3. *(proof / prove)*

   I have no ______________ that he committed the crime. Do you have any ______________? Maybe no one can ______________ it.

4. *(choose / choice / chose)*

   What courses are you going to ______________? I didn't ______________ any courses yesterday because I won't be studying this year. It is my ______________ to work instead.

5. *(then / than)*

   I think that you are taller ______________ Chantal is, but ______________ you would be, wouldn't you. You're much older ______________ she is.

6. *(all ready / already)*

   I'm ______________ to leave. I phoned Susan, and she said that everyone is ______________ there.

7. *(advice / advise)*

   Anika can't shake her depression. I tried to ______________ her to see someone, so she finally went to a therapist for ______________.

8. *(conscience / conscious)*

   Harry has been cheating on his wife for months. Doesn't he have a guilty ______________?

He must be ________________ that his wife would never accept it and would probably leave him.

9. *(past / passed)*

Claire: That bicycle ________________ right in front of me. I could have hit that person!

Alan: Well, it's over. You didn't hit him. Let the ________________ stay in the ________________

10. *(sight / cite / site)*

Rene: Have you looked at the ________________ for the Forum? I could ________________ many experts who think that the old building is still in very good condition.

Helen: I haven't seen it yet. My ________________ isn't very good any more, and I don't have my new glasses yet.

SPELLING HINT

When choosing between IE or EI combinations, English students often resort to an old rhyme:

I before E, except after C, or when sounding like "aye" as in neighbor and weigh.

EXERCISE 2

These sentences each have 1 or 2 spelling errors. Circle the misspelled words and write them correctly in the space provided.

_______ 1. That man works for the gouvernment.

_______ 2. Where did you put the reciepts?

_______ 3. You must take responsability for your actions. If you brake the law, it's your problem.

_______ 4. Is there an other way to say "cool"? That is a word wich I've been overusing.

_______ 5. The banks are realy raising the service charges a lot this year.

_______ 6. Please talk quietly! We shouldn't discuss our personel problems here.

_______ 7. Who's telephone book is that?

_______ 8. The lesson is clearly to complicated for most students.

_______ 9. I will make a thorought review of your case.

_______ 10. Mr. Alder wants to discuss the issue whit me.

_______ 11. The new employee has a nice personnality.

_______ 12. My sister, whose divorced, thinks that the institution of mariage is getting weaker.

_______ 13. Why don't you beleive me? Didn't you receive my note?

_______ 14. Harry loaded the boxes onto the frieght train.

QUIZ

Circle and correct the spelling errors in the following text.

A girl on my street named Darcy mysteriously disapeared one spring morning. It wasn't foul play. Before leaving she placed a neatly printed note on the top of her dresser. The note explained in a very polite tone that althought she appreciated the love and attention that her family was giving her, she needed to have a little time on her own, and she wanted to prouve to everyone that she could take care of herself.

According to the note, she had simply woken up that morning feeling uninspired with school and home life, and she no longer wanted to be treated like a kid. She took her savings and got on the next bus out of town. Her destination was nobody's buisiness, she went on in the letter, and she asked her family to respect her choice. After all, she stated, seventeen year olds are allowed to leave home. There is nothing ilegal about it.

I ran into Darcy, quiet by accident, on that bus trip. She was extremly calm and well dressed for her adventure. Her clothes were pressed and her nails were painted. She freely admited to me that she was going on a trip without her parents' permission. She was hoping to find a job in a good compagny, and she thougth that she'd easyly find an appartement. I was in my early twentys at the time, and I knew what awaited her. I knew that she'd need alot more schooling before she'd find that *good* job, but I also knew that she had already been given that type of advise. She would have to learn from her own experiences. I suppose that I admired her courage and confidence, and her naivity was touching.

This is a unique period to be growing up in. In the past, youths aged thirteen or fourteen were *expected* to work, to supplement the family income, and soon after, to start their own families. Now we live much longer then humans did in the past, and the *in-between* period of being neither a child nor an adult is extended. Our youths are kept in schools for a relatively long period of time and they are rarely expected to help support the familly. When youths act *wild* and rebellious, perhaps what they really need is a chance to be physically and emotionally challenged with *adult* responsability. Darcy wanted, in her own way, to forge an *adult* identity for herself.

The following question now has significance for you.
Add it to the **Technical Checklist** at the beginning of your book.

HAVE I CHECKED MY SPELLING?

SECTION 9

Gallicisms

Gallicisms are words or expressions that are used in English as they would be in French. While it is true that some French words and expressions such as *corduroy, genre, and à la carte* have been incorporated in to the English language, there are many others that have not.

In order to avoid gallicism *goof-ups,* you will have to watch out for the following:

* words that are similar in the two languages but have different spellings

Look at the following list of French words and find their English equivalents:

1. abréviation ______________________________
2. adresse ______________________________
3. appartement ______________________________
4. canadien ______________________________
5. caractère ______________________________
6. développement ______________________________
7. exagéré ______________________________
8. exemple ______________________________
9. experiences psychologiques ______________________________
10. personnes ______________________________

11. personnellement ______________________

12. futur ______________________

13. gouvernement ______________________

14. littérature ______________________

15. un scientifique ______________________

16. système ______________________

* words that are treated as **count nouns** in French but not in English

While each of the following sentences appears to be written in English, they contain glaring gallicisms.

That teacher is far too demanding of her students. Each week, she gives more and more ***homeworks.***

I was wondering if you could provide me with some ***informations*** *about your new product.*

The underlined words are **non-count nouns** in English and are never made plural. Below you will find a partial list of non-count nouns. In French, these would be considered count nouns and would take a plural form.

Abstract Concepts	***Category Nouns***
advice	baggage
confidence	cereal
evidence	equipment
health	furniture
intelligence	homework
knowledge	research
information	hair

* words that look the same in English and French but have very different meanings

Look at the following sentence examples.

*I am **actually** a student but I won't be next week because I am graduating.*
Look up the *italicized* word in the dictionary. How does it differ from the word *actuellement*?

*I am in good shape because I **practise** many sports in my spare time.*
Does *practise* mean the same thing as *pratiquer*?

* gallicisms that occur when a writer decides to use either an inappropriate French word or a direct translation of a French word when writing in English

In the following sentences, identify any French words that are being used incorrectly in English, and correct them by finding an appropriate English word.

1. I have received a good formation in computer engineering.
2. When you leave, make sure you close the lights.
3. there is an inscription fee of $29.00 for each course.
4. As part of my program, I'm doing a stage in electrical engineering.

In order to avoid all of these problems, you will need to develop a close relationship with your dictionary. If you see a word or phrase that looks or sounds even remotely French (especially if you were thinking in French when you wrote it), take the time to look it up in the dictionary to make sure that it is correct and/or appropriate in English.

EXERCISE 1

Read the following sentences and correct any gallicisms

1. The accused was found not guilty of murder because the prosecution could not find enough evidences to convict him.
2. I work at two part-time jobs so I can win enough money to pay my tuition fees.
3. Billie Holiday had all the caracteristics I like in a singer.
4. I have done a lot of interesting researches in my psychology courses.
5. I was deceived when she didn't show up for our date last Saturday night.
6. If you follow all the advices I gave you, you'll feel better in the morning.

7. My high school history professor really inspired me to be my best.
8. Your hockey bag won't close because you have too many equipments in it!
9. Teachers get paid according to their experience and their scholarity.
10. I love my Philosophy teacher. I am assisting in three of her courses this semester.
11. Maria is very sensible and cries very easily.
12. I love Florida. I think I will pass all my winters there.

FINAL QUIZ

Read the following essay. Using your Technical Checklist, identify and correct the errors.

> There was a time in history when most people lived on farms, and there lives revolved around the rules imposed by mother nature. Their activities and needs were dictate by the seasons. Children would attend school in the fall and winter because these were the seasons when labor requirements on the farm were minimal. As soon as spring approached though the children were needed to help plant seeds and to tend to crops and livestock. We now live in a society, with very different needs. Most people now live in cities, not farms, so there is no longer any reasons to continue giving students and teachers the summer off.
>
> In the modern world, the reality is that in most households, both parents work. This means that when schools send their students away on vacation in June, parents have to make other arrangements to insure that their will be supervised during the day.; Where this can be inconvenient for a household with two incomes, it is downright painful for single mothers who allready have a tough enough time making ends meet. The result of this is that many children are left to fend for themselves while their guilt-laden mothers are at work.
>
> Even those children whose parents can afford to hire someone to look after them, often spends most of their times in front of a television or complaining of boredom. In a country where it is increasingly evident that children are not learning the basic habilities they need to learn, shouldn't the gouvernment be taking these kids out of their living rooms and putting them in positive learning situations. Summer would be the perfect time to put into practice some of what the children learn during the school year. For exemple: just imagine both the personnal

and societal benefits of a child being able to see animals giving birth in the spring or to be shown how to test the cleanliness of the water in our lakes and streams.

Even if parents had to subsidize a summer-learning program, it would still cost them less then individualize day care. It would also ensure that all children, irregardless of economic status, could have equal access to adult supervision as well as intellectuel stimulation. Also, teachers would not necessarely have to give up their precious (and union protected) summer vacations. Older students could work in concert with advisors to organize and implement these programs. At a time when summer jobs are few and far between, could you imagine a better way to motivate students to learn.

As you can see, it is time to end the outdated tradition of closing schools from june to september. Times have changed, the needs of society changed and its time for the school system to change.

The following question now has significance for you.
Add it to the **Technical Checklist** at the beginning of your book.

HAVE I CHECKED TO SEE IF I USED ANY GALLICISMS?

Credits

Chapter 1

The Best Training for Real Life

Michael Korda, "The Best Training for Real Life," from *The writer's Handbook,* 1988 Edition. The Writer, Inc. Publishers. Reprinted with permission of author.

Chapter 2

Finishing School

From *I Know Why the Caged Bird Sings* by Maya Angelou. Copyright © 1969 by Maya Angelou. reprinted by permission of Random House, Inc.

Chapter 3

The Discus Thrower

Copyright © 1979 by Richard Selzer. Reprinted by permission of John Hawkins & Associates, Inc.

Do Not Go Gentle Into That Good Night

Dylan Thomas, "Do Not Go Gentle Into That Good Night" © 1953, from *The Collected Poems of Dylan Thomas,* J.M. Dent Publishers. Reprinted with permission of David Higham Associates.

Chapter 5

A Lamb to the Slaughter

Roald Dahl, "Lamb to the Slaughter," from *Someone Like You,* © 1953, Knopf. Reprinted by permission of the author and the Watkins/Loomis Agency.

Chapter 6

Monkey on My Back

Reprinted with permission of Paul Vasey.

Chapter 7

Gold Wings

Leo McKay Jr., "Gold Wings," from *Like This,* © 1995 House of Anansi Press. Reprinted with permission of Stoddart Publishing Co. Limited.

On Saint Urbain Street

Milton Acorn, "On Saint Urbain Street," from *I've Tasted My Blood,* by Milton Acorn, Ryerson Press.

Chapter 8

Bugs

Reprinted with permission of Nancy Holmes.

Chapter 9

Bad Girl

Reprinted with permission of Turnstone Press.

Rapunzel

"Rapunzel," from *The Complete Fairy Tales of the Brothers Grimm* by Jack Zipes, Translator, Translation copyright © 1987 by Jack Zipes. Used by permission of Bantam Books, a division of Bantam Doubleday Dell Publishing Group, Inc.

The Birth of Max Mueller

Cookie Mueller, "The Birth of Max Mueller—Sept. 25, 1971," from *Walking Through Clear Water in a Pool Painted Black,* Semiotexte Native Agents Series, © 1990. Reprinted with permission.

Stainless Steel Reflections

Reprinted with permission of M.J. Canuel.

Index

A
Acorn, Milton, 71
Allusion, 58
Ambiguity, 139
Angelou, Maya, 4
Antagonist, 35
Arnason, David, 91

B
Bad Girl, 91
The Best Training for Life-Fiction, 2
The Birth of Max Mueller, September 25, 1971, 95
Bugs, 76

C
Canuel, M.J., 99
Character: analyzing character, 61
  defining character, 59
  development, 49
  dynamic, 60
  static, 60
Citing references, 135
Cliché, 82
Climax, 36
Commas, 126-130
Comparison and contrast, 85
Conclusion: writing an effective conclusion, 31-34
  as an element of plot, 36
Conflict, 35
Count and non-count nouns, 152

D
Dahl, Roald, 37
Dangling modifiers, 138
Descriptive writing, 17
The Discus Thrower, 18
Do Not Go Gentle Into that Good Night, 22

E
Essay: defined, 7
  formal, 28
  planning an essay, 46
Eulogy, 71
Exposition, 36

F
Falling action, 36
Finishing School, 8
Foreshadow, 43
Fragments, 125

G
Gallicisms, 151-155
Gold Wings, 64

H
Hisstory, 28
Holmes, Nancy, 76

I
Introduction, 23-26
Irony, 4, 69

K
Korda, Michael, 2

L
Lamb to the Slaughter, 37
Literature, 1

M
McKay, Leo, 64
Metaphor, 12, 31
Misplaced modifiers, 138
Monkey On My Back, 50
Mueller, Cookie, 95

O
On St-Urbain Street, 71
Opinion writing, 27
Oral presentation, 101

P
Parallel structure, 140
Past perfect versus the simple past, 115-118
Plot, 36
Point of view, 61
Prefixes, 143
Present perfect versus the simple past, 109-113

Pronoun pitfalls, 119-124
Protagonist, 35

Q

Quotation marks, 131
Quoting from an outside source, 134

R

Rapunzel, 88
Reference page, 135
Rising action, 36
Run-On Sentences, 125

S

Selzer, Richard, 18
Semicolons, 126-130
Sentences: simple, compound, complex, 137
  problems, 137
Setting: analyzing setting, 71
  defined, 63
Short story: defined, 35
Simile, 21
Spelling pitfalls, 143
Stainless Steel Reflections, 99
Subject-verb agreement, 105-108
Suffixes, 144
Synonyms, 4

T

Taylor, Rene, 28
Theme: analyzing theme, 82-83
  defined, 75
Thesis, 12, 23
Thesis: comparison and contrast of thesis, 85
Thomas, Dylan, 22
Topic sentences, 12-16
Transitional words, 47
Transitional words: comparison and contrast, 88

V

Vasey, Paul, 50

W

Works cited, 135
Word pictures, 60